AF593416

DEPART YE

A BOOK OF PRAYER THROUGH LAMENTATIONS

By Jeremy D. Vogan

Preface

"How lonely sits the city that was full of people."

So begins the book of Lamentations, one of the most raw and real in all of Holy Scripture. Here is no subtle posturing or empty emotional manipulation, but only the outpouring of a heart caught up with the holiness of God watching the destruction of His covenant people for their sin. At first glance the postmodern American may turn the page away from this chronicle because of its darkness, but beneath the troubled waters of the Weeping Prophet's tears there is a tremendous fountain of spiritual joy to be found. There is hope in exile, there is rescue for the desolate, there is rebuke for the false prophets, there is defeat for the enemies of Judah, there is restoration for the lost, there is healing for the afflicted, there is food for the hungry, there is vindication for the silenced, there is deliverance for the downtrodden, there is comfort for those who mourn, and for those who have departed from all they once loved there is a throne that will endure to all generations. Jeremiah faces head-on some of the most heartrending griefs we can ever know, and he does it in this great conviction: That the steadfast love of the Lord never ceases; That His mercies never come to an end; That they are new every morning. Great is Thy faithfulness, Lord, unto me.

Depart Ye is a daily prayer devotional Monday through Friday for thirty-one weeks, intended to lead the believer through a season of sorrow into a deeper walk with the Lord Jesus Christ, using the Old and the New Testaments of Scripture to reveal His finished work on the Cross.

Jeremy D. Vogan
Staunton, Virginia, 2024

~MONDAY~

Lamentations 1:1 ***"How lonely sits the city that was full of people! How like a widow has she become, she who was great among the nations! She who was a princess among the provinces has become a slave."***

Cities are meant to be full, Lord

Their gates should teem with people

Their markets bursting with good things

Their houses ringing with voices of young and old

Their streets busy with children at play

Their places of worship rich with Word and prayer

Joy, gladness, hope, encouragement, praise, honor, work, play, song, dance, shouts–

Life.

But Your hand has been heavy on us, Lord. We sit empty among the cities, we who once were full of people

Like a widow who pauses from her sweeping to sadly think, and quietly mourn

We remember what we once were, what we once had, all we once did

But it is all gone now

The sparkling crown we nobly wore is cast down now; our servitude is hard now

For we have forgotten our Husband, our Maker, our Friend

Yet for all this, You have not forgotten us

And in our lament of deep sorrow

We return to You again, Lord. Amen

~TUESDAY~

Lamentations 1:2 ***"She weeps bitterly in the night, with tears on her cheeks; among all her lovers she has none to comfort her; all her friends have dealt treacherously with her; they have become her enemies."***

We once were close, Lord

Our hearts were knit together

We faced the world side by side; we tasted the joys and sorrows of life

The beauty of friendship became our highest good; the joy of affinity, our highest truth

But in between every human relationship, there must be actual spiritual truth. There must be a true Mediator

And we exchanged that truth for a lie

The lie that we could worship and serve the creature rather than the Creator

Who is blessed forever! Amen

And the cost of that lie is staggering

The righteous Law has exacted losses as we have deviated from Your will

You have toppled the idols of faithless friendship and false intimacy in our hearts

And we are left weeping bitterly in the night

Yet we are not left alone. For there is a Friend who sticks closer than a brother

And He has prepared a table for me in the midst of my enemies

He anoints my head with oil; my cup overflows

Surely goodness and mercy shall follow me all the days of my life

And I shall dwell in the house of the Lord forever. Amen

~WEDNESDAY~

Lamentations 1:3 "Judah has gone into exile because of affliction and hard servitude; she dwells now among the nations, but finds no resting place; her pursuers have all overtaken her in the midst of her distress."

Once we dwelt among Your people, Lord

Jerusalem – built as a city that is bound firmly together

To which the tribes go up, the tribes of the Lord

As was decreed for Israel

To give thanks to the Name of the Lord

Have we forgotten Your Name? Was Your glory not our highest good? Yet here we are, far from our resting place

Here we are in exile

Our only comfort Your Word that still speaks

Our only guide Your Spirit who still indwells

Our only hope Your promises that are still true

Our only desire Your presence that is still here, even in this desolate place

Our only longing to return to You, wherever that may take us, whatever it may cost

For the place we left behind was dear to us. Yet it was not the place itself that we loved, Lord; it was You

Meet with us here, in the midst of our sorrow and our distress

Show us Your glory, encourage our hearts, confront our sin, establish our prayers

Teach us never to depart from You again

And beyond the veil, into eternity, give us a glimpse of Home. Amen

~THURSDAY~

Lamentations 1:4 "The roads to Zion mourn, for none come to the festival; all her gates are desolate; all her priests groan; her virgins have been afflicted, and she herself suffers bitterly."

ll Creation groans, Lord. The earth that You set on its foundations, that it should never be moved; the deep You covered as with a garment

The mountains that rose, the valleys that sank down to the place that You appointed for them

The springs You made to gush forth in the valleys, flowing between the hills, that give drink to every beast of the field; the wild donkeys quench their thirst

Beside them the birds of the heavens dwell; they sing among the branches. These all look to You, to give them their food in due season

When You give it to them, they gather it up; when You open Your hand, they are filled with good things

When You hide Your face, they are dismayed; when You take away their breath, they die and return to their dust

All this we were to have been stewards over. And when we fell from our high place, and were made desolate for our sin against You

This world fell with us, and ceased to be very good, as You had made it

So Your Spirit draws our eyes away from the empty roads, the abandoned festival, the desolate gates

And through bitter suffering we are shown a new vision: The Lord of Hosts with us, the God of Jacob as our fortress. *Selah*

God is our refuge and strength, our very present help in trouble

Therefore we will not fear though the earth gives way and the mountains be moved into the heart of the sea

God is in the midst of us, we shall not be moved; God will help us when morning dawns. Amen

~FRIDAY~

Lamentations 1:5 "Her foes have become the head; her enemies prosper, because the Lord has afflicted her for the multitude of her transgressions; her children have gone away, captives before the foe."

Every word of Yours, O God, proves true; You are a shield to all those who take refuge in You

You promised that if we faithfully obeyed the voice of the Lord our God, being careful to do all His commandments, the Lord our God would set us high above all the nations of the earth

And all these blessings would come upon us and overtake us: We would be blessed in the city, and blessed in the field

Blessed would be the fruit of our womb and the fruit of the ground and the fruit of our cattle, the increase of our herds and the young of our flock

Blessed would be our basket and our kneading bowl; blessed would we be when we came in, and when we went out

The Lord would cause our enemies to come out against us one way, and flee from us seven ways. But we did not obey the voice of the Lord, and were not careful to do all His commandments; every word of Yours proved true

Jesus Christ stepped in and took curses, confusion, and frustration on Himself, for us. He was cursed in the city, and cursed in the field, a horror to all the kingdoms of the earth

The heavens over His head were bronze, and the earth under Him was iron; the rain of His land was powder, and a wasting disease was set upon Him

A hard-faced nation came swooping down and took Him away, until He was destroyed

But who can speak of His generation? For He saw the light of life, and was satisfied

Every Word of Yours proves true; You are a shield to all those who take refuge in You

Amen

~MONDAY~

Lamentations 1:6 "From the daughter of Zion all her majesty has departed. Her princes have become deer that find no pasture; they fled without strength before the pursuer."

As the leaders go, Lord, so goes the church. You have made us to be a community

A people to be called by Your Name, hearts united in common purpose

Known by our love

Defined by Your Word

Hungering and thirsting for righteousness

Governed by grace, led by the Spirit

But we are not. *Ichabod* You have called us, for the glory has departed from Israel

We are alone in the crowd, among all who have turned away from You

I have followed Paul, you have followed Apollos

Divided amongst ourselves–though Christ is not divided

Lovers of self

Tongues set on fire, a world of unrighteousness

Not seeking the wisdom that is from above, but earthly, unspiritual, demonic

A law unto ourselves, the desires of our flesh warring against the Spirit

Show us, Lord, that we have never had any glory at all, in anything or anyone, save in You

That Jesus Christ is our shield, our very great reward. Whom shall we fear?

For You we will wait in silence, Lord. Amen

~TUESDAY~

Lamentations 1:7a "Jerusalem remembers in the days of her affliction and wandering all the precious things that were hers from days of old."

There was a time, Lord

When we walked in the sun, bathed in the warmth of Your presence

When it seemed we could do no wrong

When those who opposed us were ashamed, for Your Name was on us

When we delighted to go to the house of worship, lifting our voices together in harmony

Praising You for Your steadfast love

Beseeching You to hear us

Armed with the Cross

Braved to suffer toil or loss

Counting earthly gain but dross

What did it all mean? Was any of it real? Did it truly honor You?

Surely it was, Lord, it did. Yet it was only a season

Seasons come, and seasons go. You, and You alone, endure forever

Teach us to keep our eyes on You:

The only one who was still with us in the days of our affliction

The only one who still remembers us

The only one who has been our Savior from the days of old, and still calls us by Your Name

You are our great and only hope, Lord. Amen

~WEDNESDAY~

Lamentations 1:7b "When her people fell into the hand of the foe, and there was none to help her, her foes gloated over her; they mocked at her downfall."

There was none to help us, Lord

We knew the Day was coming

Your holy Word foretold the just punishment for our sin

Your faithful prophets proclaimed it

Our consciences smote us every time we sacrificed under a spreading tree and on a high hill

We did not remember the warnings of Your covenant

We did not heed the signs in the heavens, the rumblings in the earth

When the enemy burst through the gates, we were without defense

For there was nothing to be said, nothing to be done. Only sadness and repentance

The memory of Your grace and goodness to us only served as condemnation

To exile we went, bowed down in sorrow

To hard labor, remembering how You delivered us from the land of slavery

To bitter loss, and a long corridor of guilt and shame

Yet You did not gloat, or mock at our downfall

You took all of it on Yourself, and stepped into our place

The exile, the labor, the loss, the shame. All of it

Our sins have been removed from us as far as the east is from the west; glory!

Lord Jesus, I owe you all I have, everything I am, that which I hope for. Teach me never to leave Your blessed presence again. Amen

~THURSDAY~

Lamentations 1:8 "Jerusalem sinned grievously; therefore she became filthy; all who honored her despise her, for they have seen her nakedness; she herself groans and turns her face away."

We have lost something, Lord. An innocence

A childlike acceptance of Your words; a holy fear in Your presence

A sincere alarm at sin

Not from duty, as ones who must keep Your Law or perish

But from love, as ones who owe You everything–even our own selves

We have lost our faithfulness, which we pledged You on the day You made us Your own

Our purity

Our dedication to You, the unswerving heart-worship we offered in Your holy temple

Our joy, our righteousness in Your presence. And in our affliction we are brought to this place

Your own people, called by Your Name, groaning and turning our face away from our sin

It has cost us more than we could ever repay

We come, then, to thc only One who can, who has, who will

You are the source of all true holiness, all purity, all love, all truth, all faithfulness, all joy

For You alone, Lord, we wait in silence, holding up all it is we have to offer You:

Our hearts. By the grace and mercy of Jesus Christ we implore You, meet us here. Amen

~FRIDAY~

Lamentations 1:9 "Her uncleanness was in her skirts; she took no thought of her future; therefore her fall is terrible; she has no comforter. O Lord, behold my affliction, for the enemy has triumphed!"

There is nothing left, Lord. Our sin has exacted more than we can make good

More than we can know

More than we can reckon with

More than we can atone for

More even than we are, or have to offer

Sins we have committed, yet even our death would not repay

Sins against Your holiness, against Your goodness

A betrayal of all that You created good

An undermining of Your sovereign will

A wicked rebellion against all You have done for us

Shame and regret are our future, and our fall is terrible

Until–

Until Jesus Christ stepped into our place

Until He took our punishment and drained to the dregs the cup of Your holy wrath

Until He fulfilled every word in the Law and satisfied everything it required

Until He said, *"It is finished,"* and bowed His head, and gave up His spirit

Mercy triumphed over judgment, and we were cleansed from our former sins

Lord, I owe you everything. Lead me in Your ways today. Amen.

~MONDAY~

Lamentations 1:10 "The enemy has stretched out his hands over all her precious things; for she has seen the nations enter her sanctuary, those whom you forbade to enter your congregation."

Who can ascend Your holy hill, Lord? Who will stand in Your holy place?

He who has clean hands and a pure heart, who does not lift up his soul to what is false, and does not swear deceitfully

He will receive blessing from the Lord, and righteousness from the God of his salvation

Such is the generation of those who seek You

Who seek Your face, O God of Jacob

Who is it that has done all these things? Who is the generation of those who seek You?

It is You alone

Yours are the clean hands, which have wronged no one

Yours the pure heart, dedicated unswervingly to the true worship of God the Father

Your soul lifted up to the Lord, in whom alone You trusted

Truly, truly, You said unto us: *The poor in spirit are blessed of God, for theirs is the Kingdom of Heaven*

We are Your generation, Lord Jesus

We who used to be Your enemies, who once were far off, but now brought near by the blood of Christ

Found in You, not having our own righteousness, but that which is through faith

We will praise You forever. Amen

~TUESDAY~

Lamentations 1:11 "All her people groan as they search for bread; they trade their treasures for food to revive their strength. 'Look, O Lord, and see, for I am despised.'"

Once there was plenty, Lord, more than we could even give thanks for

There was rich food for the eating

Welcoming homes with open doors

Friends with open hearts, work that fulfilled our calling

A community that together lifted our worship to You

Enemies that showed their faces openly

A dawn that was full of promise. But the day is long spent now, and much has changed

There is want

The corners of the fields are bare. Doors are closed, shades are drawn

Hurt and disappointment keep Your people far apart from each other

Thorns and thistles have overtaken our harvest

We feel divided, despairing, defeated

A man's foes those of his own household

A night that comes with no blessing

And at last we know, as we did not know before:

That this world is not, can never be, our everlasting home

That Christ has taken the full measure of Your wrath on Him

Is there any sorrow like unto His sorrow? On Jesus Christ alone is our hope. Amen

~WEDNESDAY~

Lamentations 1:12 "Is it nothing to you, all you who pass by? Look and see if there is any sorrow like my sorrow, which was brought upon me, which the Lord inflicted on the day of his fierce anger."

Why does the sorrow run so deep, Lord? Why do the memories cut so keenly

The days when we used to gather in Your Name for worship

When unity and truth walked so closely together

When our strength was used against error, against evil, against waywardness; and not against each other

When wisdom spoke from Your Word, and together we yielded our hearts to it

When Your Spirit prompted, and as one we offered ourselves

Your people offered ourselves freely on the day of Your power

In holy garments, from the womb of the morning

The dew of our youth was Yours

But the Lord was at our right hand, shattering kings on the Day of Your wrath

Executing judgment among the nations, filling them with the dead

And when You drank from the brook, and lifted up Your head

You had purified Your own, and costly indeed was that purification

Holiness was the fruit You sought, and Your own image the true reflection

I know, now, why the sorrow runs so deep: Because I loved them

And I know why I serve the Lord with fear: Because Christ loved me, and gave Himself for me

Whom have I in Heaven but You? But God is the strength of my heart forever. Amen

~THURSDAY~

Lamentations 1:13 "From on high he sent fire; into my bones he made it descend; he spread a net for my feet; he turned me back; he has left me stunned, faint all the day long."

There is a judgment, Lord, a reckoning for our evil deeds

A day when our careless words are echoed back to us again

When the pain we caused to others becomes our own; when the senseless wars we perpetrated are inflicted on those we love

When the forest set ablaze by our tongues surrounds us, with no escape

When our riches have rotted and our garments are moth-eaten

Our gold and silver turn on us, to eat our own flesh like fire; the treasure we have laid up for ourselves in the last days rises up to cry out against us

Behold, the cries of the defrauded harvesters who mowed our fields have reached the ears of the Lord of Hosts, and He is coming to judge the living and the dead

We have fattened our hearts in the day of slaughter, and condemned and murdered the righteous Person, and He has not resisted us

And to our dismay we have looked on the One we have pierced. You took the judgment for our evil deeds; You took the shame of our careless words

The pain and devastation of our sins was laid upon You, and You took the punishment for them. The corrosion and betrayal of our riches fell upon You

And in their stead You have faithfully offered us blessing, eternal life, the smile of Your Father

Christ redeemed us from the curse of the Law by becoming a curse for us, for it is written, *"Cursed is everyone who is hanged on a tree"*

So that we might receive the promised Spirit by faith. What a salvation! What a mighty exchange! What hope in the midst of despair, Lord.

What a Savior! Lord Jesus, help me to proclaim Your glories today

Amen

~FRIDAY~

Lamentations 1:14 "My transgressions were bound into a yoke; by his hand they were fastened together, they were set upon my neck; he caused my strength to fail; the Lord gave me into the hands of those whom I cannot withstand."

Sin is too heavy, Lord. We cannot bear the weight of it

It destroyed the innocence of our parents in the Garden

It brought death on the heads of every human being

It banished Adam and Eve from Your presence; it set a flaming sword between them and the Tree of Life

So that Death would have to be conquered before they could taste of it

It flared up in Cain's heart, and drove him to murder his brother. The blood cried out from the ground against him, and he was cursed to wander the earth

It drove a wedge between Ishmael and Isaac, between the child of slavery and the child of promise

It pitted Jacob and Esau against each other as they strove for the blessing

And for more than a thousand years it would prove, beyond any doubt, that the blood of bulls and goats could not sanctify to the purifying of the flesh

Even the holy Law could not deliver from sin; all it could ever do was condemn. And when the Lord Christ bore sin for all His own, yea, even became sin for our sake, the waves of death went over His head

Yet He rose again in the power of an indestructible life, and ascended into glory. Alleluia! Who shall bring any charge against God's elect? It is God who justifies

Who is to condemn? Christ Jesus is the one who died and more than that, who was raised, who stands at God's right hand to intercede for us

Who shall separate us from the love of Christ? Shall tribulation, or distress, or persecution? No, in all these things we are more than conquerors through Him who loved us. Amen

~MONDAY~

Lamentations 1:15 "The Lord rejected all my mighty men in my midst; he summoned an assembly against me to crush my young men; the Lord has trodden as in a winepress the virgin daughter of Judah."

The young, the strong, and the beautiful, Lord; all that is worshiped by the world

The young are unscourged by the ravages of time

The strong are untouched by the attacks of our enemies

The beautiful are admirable in their own right; they need no downward glance of humility

They have won; they have achieved all we ever longed for

But have they, really? Is that the truth? For the innocence of youth fades in its very flower, and is displaced by regret

Strength fails one day, and there is a breach in the wall–in every wall

Beauty withers, and the more tightly it is grasped, the more surely it turns back to dust: The dust we were made from, the dust of the very earth

We put to death, therefore, whatever is earthly in us: Sexual immorality, impurity, passion, evil desire, and covetousness, which is idolatry

On account of these the wrath of God is coming

Here there is no Greek and Jew, circumcised and uncircumcised, barbarian, Scythian, slave, free; but Christ is all, and in all

We put on then, as God's chosen ones, holy and beloved, compassionate hearts, kindness, humility, meekness, and patience, bearing with one another and, if one has a complaint against another, forgiving each other

As the Lord has forgiven us, so we also must forgive; and above all these we put on love, which binds everything together in perfect harmony

The Word of Christ dwells in us richly, and in Your presence we will praise You forever

Amen

~TUESDAY~

Lamentations 1:16 "For these things I weep; my eyes flow with tears; for a comforter is far from me, one to revive my spirit; my children are desolate, for the enemy has prevailed."

Some days the waves go over my head, Lord

It seems like everything goes wrong

Like all that I touch turns to ashes

Like failure has permanently replaced success

Like loss is the way things are now

Like sadness has utterly triumphed over joy

Like my children are desolate, for the enemy has prevailed over us

A voice is heard in Ramah, lamentation and bitter weeping

It is Rachel weeping for her children

And refusing to be comforted, for they are no more

Is there a reward for my work? Shall they come back from the land of the enemy?

The Lord gives the word; the women who announce the news are a great host

"The kings of the armies–they flee, they flee!"

The wings of the dove are covered with silver; its pinions with shimmering gold

When the Almighty scatters kings there, let snow fall on Zalmon

O kingdoms of the earth, sing to God

Sing praises to the Lord! *Selah*

Blessed be the Lord, who daily bears us up. God is our salvation. *Selah.* Amen

~WEDNESDAY~

Lamentations 1:17 "Zion stretches out her hands, but there is none to comfort her; the Lord has commanded against Jacob that his neighbors should be his foes; Jerusalem has become a filthy thing among them."

What do you do with sorrow, Lord? What do you do with loss

Friends are many when the sun is shining

Brothers and sisters are close around you when things are going well

Wealth attracts many, as your Proverbs, but even the close friend of the poor deserts them

Yet this is the wisdom You taught:

Blessed are you who are poor, for yours is the Kingdom of God

Blessed are you who are hungry now, for you shall be satisfied

Blessed are you who weep now, for you shall laugh

Woe to you who are rich, for you have received your consolation

Woe to you who are full now, for you shall be hungry

Woe to you who laugh now, for you shall mourn and weep

Woe to you, when all people speak well of you, for so their fathers did to the false prophets

See, Lord, we have left everything to follow You. We have become like the scum of the world, the refuse of all things

In the new world, when the Son of Man will sit on His glorious throne, You have promised us to receive a hundredfold, and to inherit eternal life

Yet for all this, it is for Your sake alone that we have suffered the loss of all things, in order that we may gain Christ and be found in You

To know You and the power of Your Resurrection. May it be, Lord Jesus. Amen

~THURSDAY~

Lamentations 1:18 "The Lord is in the right, for I have rebelled against his word; but hear, all you peoples, and see my suffering; my young women and my young men have gone into captivity."

Let God be true, and every man a liar

You are in the right, Lord

My rebellion against Your Word has been my downfall; there is no other reason

All the excuses I come up with fade away, even as I make them

I have not regarded lightly Your discipline, nor been weary when reproved by You

For the Lord disciplines the one He loves, and chastises every son whom He receives

I know You see our suffering, the cruel captivity we have cried out under

You have known our sorrow; You have borne our punishment

Your own Son, Your innocent Son, bore our penalty for rebellion against Your Word

Though He had obeyed it without fail

Your Son went into captivity and took the yoke of bondage upon Him

He was oppressed, and He was afflicted, yet He opened not His mouth

He who knew no sin became sin, that we might become the righteousness of God

For such a great salvation, I will proclaim it among my people; with joy I will make known among those in exile that there is a King among us again

The wounds of love are on His hands and feet, and on His side; but He has crushed the head of Death forever

The Lord is in the right; let us return again to worship Him. Amen

~FRIDAY~

Lamentations 1:19 "I called to my lovers, but they deceived me; my priests and elders perished in the city, while they sought food to revive their strength."

Our own hearts deceive us, Lord

We seek out all those who flatter us most readily

Who seem the most beautiful, the most accomplished, the most joyful, the most successful

Who thread their way most easily through this sharp-cornered world, as we long to do ourselves

And we bind our gaze to them, as to brilliant lights that rise in the sky at night

But soon or late, every one of them has fallen, their fiery course traced across the dark globe of all our deepest hopes and longings

Where is the wise man? Where is the scribe? Where is the disputer of this world?

Has not God made foolish the wisdom of this world?

For Jews demand signs and Greeks seek wisdom, but we preach Christ crucified, a stumbling block to Jews and folly to Gentiles

Therefore Your prophets shall no more see false visions or practice divination

You will deliver Your people out of their hand

And we shall know that You, and You alone, are the Lord

Scarcely had I passed them, when I found Him whom my soul loves. And I held Him, and would not let Him go

No, but even more truly–He holds me, and will never let me go

Whom have I in Heaven but You, Lord? Lead me in Your most holy way today. Amen.

~MONDAY~

Lamentations 1:20 "Look, O Lord, for I am in distress; my stomach churns; my heart is wrung within me, because I have been very rebellious. In the street the sword bereaves; in the house it is like death."

Surely there is no better indicator of the depth of our faithlessness, Lord, than that we grow tired of hearing about our sin

Yet Your holy Word continues to confront us

We have taken our idols into our hearts, Lord. We have set the stumbling block of our iniquity before our faces

We have added to the command of Your Word, and we have taken away from it

We have not kept or done Your statutes and Your rules, for that would have been our wisdom and our understanding

What was spoken to us out of the midst of the fire, when we heard the sound of words, but there was no form; there was only a Voice

We have acted corruptly by making a carved image for ourselves, in the image of created things. We have raised our eyes to heaven, and been drawn away in our hearts to worship the sun and moon and stars

We have forgotten the covenant of the Lord God who brought us out of the iron furnace of Egypt

Heaven and earth have been called to witness against us, and we have been scattered among the peoples. There we have served gods of wood and stone, the work of human hands, that neither see, nor hear, nor eat, nor smell

Did any people ever hear the voice of a god speaking out of the midst of the fire, and live? Or has any god ever attempted to take a nation for himself from the midst of another nation, by trials, by signs, by wonders, and by war, all of which the Lord did for us in Egypt?

For You are a merciful God, and have not treated us as our sins deserve.

In the person of Jesus Christ You took our Lawful punishment on Yourself. The Lord is our strength and our song, and has become our salvation. Amen

~TUESDAY~

Lamentations 1:21 "They heard my groaning, yet there is no one to comfort me. All my enemies have heard of my trouble; they are glad that you have done it. You have brought the day you announced; now let them be as I am."

With sorrow and suffering, Lord, You have stirred up my mind

Stirred up my sincere mind by way of reminder: That I should remember the predictions of the prophets and the commandment of the Lord and Savior through the apostles:

You put enmity between the serpent and the woman, and between his offspring and her offspring; He would crush his head, and he would bruise His heel

The pagan prophet saw Him, but not now; he beheld Him, but not near. A star would come out of Jacob, and a scepter rise out of Israel

He was Your Son, and You became His Father. He would ask of You, and You would make the nations His inheritance, the ends of the earth His possession

Here was Your Servant, whom You upheld; Your chosen One, in Whom You delighted. You put Your Spirit on Him to bring justice to the nations

He was despised and rejected by men, a Man of Sorrows and acquainted with grief. He was pierced for our transgressions, He was crushed for our iniquities; upon Him was the chastisement that brought us peace, and with His wounds we are healed

All we like sheep have gone astray; we have turned–every one–to his own way, and the Lord has laid on Him the iniquity of us all

All my enemies are glad that You have done it. Death, sin, and the devil: they rejoice over Him

But we do not overlook this one fact, that with the Lord one day is as a thousand years, and a thousand years as a day. Then comes the end, when He delivers the Kingdom to God the Father after destroying every rule and authority and power

For He must reign until He has put all His enemies under His feet; and the last enemy to be destroyed is Death. And according to Your promise I wait for a new heavens and a new earth. Amen

~WEDNESDAY~

Lamentations 1:22 "Let all their evildoing come before you, and deal with them as you have dealt with me because of all my transgressions; for my groans are many, and my heart is faint."

Lord, how can You look on all

How can You perceive all hearts, to know our sorrows, and hear our cries before You

How did you take on flesh? You who, though You were in the form of God, did not count equality with God a thing to be grasped

But emptied Yourself by taking the form of a servant, being born in the likeness of men

How did You see us trapped in sin, in bondage to our own evil desires, unable to bear up under the weight of our wrongdoing against You

Lost in bitterness, in wrath, in anger, clamor, slander, and all malice

And You took the punishment for all of this, all on Yourself, Lord Jesus

All our evildoing came before You: Our betrayals, our unfaithfulness, our unbelief, our rebellions, our disobedience, our failures

As an innocent sacrifice, You took the burden of all this on the Cross

God the Father dealt with You as He would have dealt with us

Because of all our transgressions, the flood of punishment for sin went over Your head

And in their stead, we are credited with Your righteousness

I stand amazed for very grace; I bless Your Name before the people, and lift high Your praise

To You who love us and have freed us from our sins by Your blood, and made us a Kingdom, priests to Your God and Father

To You be glory and dominion forever and ever. Amen

~THURSDAY~

Lamentations 2:1 "How the Lord in his anger has set the daughter of Zion under a cloud! He has cast down from heaven to earth the splendor of Israel; he has not remembered his footstool in the day of his anger."

The day has come, Lord; it has finally come

The day Your prophets warned us about: A day of thick darkness, distress, and gloom

Bind up the testimony; seal the teaching among the disciples

I will wait for the Lord, who is hiding His face from the house of Jacob, and I will hope in Him

Behold, I and the children the Lord has given me are signs and portents in Israel from the Lord of Hosts, who dwells on Mount Zion

And when they say to you, *"Inquire of the mediums and necromancers who chirp and mutter"*

Should not a people inquire of their God? Should they inquire of the dead on behalf of the living?

To the Law and to the testimony! If they will not speak according to this Word, it is because they have no dawn

They will pass through the land, greatly distressed and hungry, and they will look to the earth, but behold, distress and darkness, the gloom of anguish

They will look on Him they have pierced, and mourn for Him

Yet He will give them His own flesh for true food, and His blood for true drink

They will draw near to Him, and drink from the spiritual Rock, which is Christ

By faith they will live forever, for He will raise them up at the Last Day. God has cast down from Heaven to earth the splendor of Israel, but has glorified the Son of Man

The words that You speak to us are Spirit and life, Lord. Satisfy our deepest longings in You today. Amen

~FRIDAY~

Lamentations 2:2 "The Lord has swallowed up without mercy all the habitations of Jacob; in his wrath he has broken down the strongholds of the daughter of Judah; he has brought down to the ground in dishonor the kingdom and its rulers."

Lord, Your pronouncement has come down. All the habitations of Jacob You have swallowed up without mercy

He who left his father and mother with Your blessing upon him

Who left the birthright in Your hands, when his brother plotted to kill him;

Who stayed in Haran, after sunset, and took a stone to put under his head

Who slept and dreamed of a great stair set up on the earth, and the top of it reached to Heaven. And behold, the angels of God were ascending and descending on it!

And the Lord said, *"I am the Lord, the God of Abraham your father and the God of Isaac. The land on which you lie I will give to you and to your offspring; in you and your offspring shall all the families of the earth be blessed*

"Behold, I am with you and will keep you wherever you go, and will bring you back to this land."

Then Jacob awoke from his sleep and was afraid, and said, *"How awesome is this place! This is none other than the house of God, and this is the gate of Heaven"*

In the morning he took the stone and set it up for a pillar, and poured oil on top. And he called the name of that place Bethel, the House of God

Therefore, holy brothers, you who share in a heavenly calling, consider Jesus, the apostle and high priest of our confession

For every house is built by someone, but the builder of all things is God

And Christ is faithful over God's house as a son, who has taken all the righteous punishment of the Law on Himself

And we are His house, if indeed we hold fast our confidence and our boasting in our hope. Amen

~MONDAY~

Lamentations 2:3 "He has cut down in fierce anger all the might of Israel; he has withdrawn from them his right hand in the face of the enemy; he has burned like a flaming fire in Jacob, consuming all around."

If our God is a consuming fire–

If You truly are the Light of the World–

Then when You said, *"Let there be light"*, it was separated from darkness forever

When You led Your people out of bondage in a pillar of fire, they were delivered; when lightning flashed and smoke rose on the holy mountain, Your Law was given

The temple lights burned as all who ministered by night blessed Your Name

Your Word was given as a lamp to our feet and a light to our path; the Light of Israel became a fire, and his Holy One a flame

The people walking in darkness have seen a great light; those who dwelt in a land of deep darkness, on them has light shone

Arise, shine, for your light has come; the glory of the Lord has risen upon you!

And this is the judgment: The Light has come into the world, and people loved the darkness rather than the light, because their works were evil. But the Light shines in the darkness, and the darkness has not overcome it

The night is far gone; the Day is at hand. So then let us cast off the works of darkness and put on the armor of light

The heavens will pass away with a roar, and the heavenly bodies melt as they burn, and the earth and the works that are done on it will be exposed

Therefore, beloved, let us be diligent to be found by Him without spot or blemish, and at peace. Awake, O sleeper, arise from the dead, and Christ will shine on you

In that City which has no need of sun or moon to shine on it, for its lamp is the Lamb. Come quickly, Lord Jesus. Amen

~TUESDAY~

Lamentations 2:4 "He has bent his bow like an enemy, with his right hand set like a foe; and he has killed all who were delightful in our eyes in the tent of the daughter of Zion; he has poured out his fury like fire."

Lord, You have shown me this:

That every person should be quick to hear

Slow to speak

Slow to anger

For the anger of man does not produce the righteousness of God

To put away all filthiness and rampant wickedness, and receive with meekness the implanted Word, which is able to save our souls

There is only One who is holy

Who has given the perfect Law

Who is a faultless example of what is right and good

Who can be angry at sin, and in His anger sin not

Who can bend the bow of justice, and pour out His fury like fire

Who will one day call all things to account

To set all things right

And purify His people once for all with His holy sacrifice

A sacrifice of meekness, and submission to the Father's will

He alone is worthy, for He has drunk to its dregs the cup of the wrath of the Lord

All that was delightful of the world, of sin, of the flesh has been killed in our hearts now

We have set our eyes upon Jesus, and we will follow Him into eternity. Amen

~WEDNESDAY~

Lamentations 2:5 "The Lord has become like an enemy; he has swallowed up Israel; he has swallowed up all its palaces; he has laid in ruins its strongholds, and he has multiplied in the daughter of Judah mourning and lamentation."

Gone are the days, Lord, when we used to work together for Your Kingdom; when palaces and strongholds rose up around us, displays of Your beauty and protection

When our valiant ones went out to the enemy and were victorious over them

When king and subject worshiped You together, and the priests blessed them; when the seers spoke Your Word, and all trembled at it

When harvests were plentiful and wine flowed without measure; when the mounds of wheat overswept the storehouses

The beasts of the field nursed their young, and their numbers multiplied for us

All trembled at Your banners over us, for we were the people of the living God

How could it all be gone? Yet it is, it has been, from the day when we forgot You

When pride and evil desire ruled in our hearts instead of humble devotion; when prophets spoke what would please the people, and not what was true

When priests profaned Your holy temple with strange fire; when the king did not defend our walls, but brought his power to bear instead on the least of these, and defenseless they cried out to You

When the fields ceased to bear fruit, and the creatures stumbled into darkness, and the ruins of what was once a great city stood mute testaments to Ichabod

For what do we wait then? But You still fulfill Your Word

A Child born, a Son given, on Whose shoulder shall be the government

Over the people living in darkness You have sent out Your light, by the zeal of the Lord of hosts. You are our Wonderful Counselor, Mighty God, Everlasting Father, Prince of Peace. Amen

~THURSDAY~

Lamentations 2:6 "He has laid waste his booth like a garden, laid in ruins his meeting place; the Lord has made Zion forget festival and Sabbath, and in his fierce indignation has spurned king and priest."

It is Your Temple that is laid waste, Lord, Your holy things that have been profaned

Your commands that have been disobeyed

Your kings that have ruled falsely

Your priests that have sacrificed in the high places

Your people that have gone astray

Your Law that has been broken; Your Word that has come to pass

For did You not promise that just as all the good things You promised Israel were fulfilled, so all the evil things would surely be brought upon us if we would not love the Lord our God?

It is a great sickness within us. Yet for those with eyes of faith, it is not an illness that leads to death; it is for the glory of God, that the Son of God may be glorified through it

If anyone walks in the day, he does not stumble, because he sees this world's light

"I am the Resurrection and the Life. Whoever believes in Me, though he die, yet shall he live. And everyone who lives and believes in Me shall never die. Do you believe this?"

Yes, Lord, I believe that You are the Christ, the Son of God, who is coming into the world

See how You loved him! Yet the stone is rolled away, and the dead is raised to life

You have spurned king and priest, for You are the true royalty, the only divinity

Our empty rituals are forgotten, and by Your Spirit we worship You in truth. Amen

~FRIDAY~

Lamentations 2:7 "The Lord has scorned his altar, disowned his sanctuary; he has delivered into the hand of the enemy the walls of her palaces; they raised a clamor in the house of the Lord as on the day of festival."

Hear this, you elders; give ear, all inhabitants of the land! Has such a thing happened in your days, or in the days of your fathers?

Tell your children of it, and let your children tell their children

What the cutting locust left the swarming locust has eaten; what the swarming locust left the hopping locust has eaten; and what the hopping locust left the destroying locust has eaten

Awake, you drunkards, and weep! Wail, all you drinkers of wine, for it is cut off from your mouth

The grain offering and the drink offering are cut off from the house of the Lord; the priests mourn; the fields are destroyed and the ground mourns

Alas for the day! For the Day of the Lord is near, and as destruction from the Almighty it comes

The hour has come for the Son of Man to be glorified. *"Truly, truly,"* You said to us, *"unless a grain of wheat falls into the earth and dies, it remains alone*

"But if it dies, it bears much fruit." Whoever loves his life loses it, and whoever hates his life in this world will keep it for eternal life

If anyone serves You, he must follow You; and where You are, there will Your servant be also

As the sinless sacrifice, Lord Jesus, You were scorned; as the only Holy One, You were disowned

You were delivered into the hand of Your enemies, and they rejoiced over You when You fell

But this is a trustworthy saying: If we have died with You, we will also live with You

At Your feet we will cast our crowns, O Lord, our Rock and our Redeemer. Amen

~MONDAY~

Lamentations 2:8 "The Lord determined to lay in ruins the wall of the daughter of Zion; he stretched out the measuring line; he did not restrain his hand from destroying; he caused rampart and wall to lament; they languished together."

When You have determined Your will, O Lord, it comes to pass

You who wrote Creation's story can write its end

You who laid the foundations of the world can break them up again, by the power of Your Word

You who parted land and sea can determine where its proud waves will halt

You who set apart Your covenant people can call them to account

Understand, O dullest of the people! Fools, when will you be wise?

He who planted the ear, does He not hear? He who formed the eye, does He not see?

He who disciplines the nations, does He not rebuke? He who teaches man knowledge–the Lord–knows the thoughts of a man, that they are but a breath

The Lord, the Sovereign over all things, did not only ordain destruction

He took on flesh, in the fullness of time, the Godhead veiled in flesh, yet without sin

He lived a sinless life and died an innocent death for the sake of love, and He stepped into the destruction and took it on Himself, to ransom a people

A people whose rampart and wall would not be of this world, whose righteousness would be by faith from first to last, lest any should boast

For as in Adam all die, even so in Christ shall all be made alive

So we are found in Him as new Creation: The old has gone, the new has come

And this is eternal life, that we know You, the only true God, and Jesus Christ whom You have sent. Amen

~TUESDAY~

Lamentations 2:9 "Her gates have sunk into the ground; he has ruined and broken the bars; her king and princes are among the nations; the law is no more, and her prophets find no vision from the Lord."

In the seventh month, Lord, on the twenty-first day of the month, the Word of the Lord came by the hand of Haggai the prophet

To Zerubbabel the governor, and to Joshua the high priest:

"Who is left among you who saw this house in its former glory? How do you see it now; is it not as nothing in your eyes?

Yet now be strong, O Zerubbabel; be strong, O Joshua the high priest; be strong, all you people of the land

Work, for I am with you," declares the Lord of hosts, *"according to the covenant that I made with you when you came out of Egypt*

"My Spirit remains in your midst. Fear not"

For thus says the Lord of hosts: *"Yet once more, in a little while, I will shake the heavens and the earth and the sea and the dry land*

And I will shake all nations, so that the Desire of the Nations shall come

And I will fill this house with glory"

Whose shall be the silver in this house, Lord, and whose the gold? Whose but Yours?

The latter glory of this house shall be greater than the former; in this house You shall at last give us peace

For Jesus Christ has been counted worthy of more glory than the giver of the Law

And we are His House, if indeed we hold fast our confidence and our boasting in our hope

Be silent, all flesh, before the Lord, for He has roused Himself from His holy dwelling. Amen.

~WEDNESDAY~

Lamentations 2:10 "The elders of the daughter of Zion sit on the ground in silence; they have thrown dust on their heads and put on sackcloth; the young women of Jerusalem have bowed their heads to the ground."

Where is wisdom, Lord?

Where is beauty

Where is faithfulness to be found

Who is to be found worthy? What knowledge endures

Can we find anything that has not crumbled, a firm place to stand?

Shall anyone or anything be judged faultless before You?

They have all passed away

Like water under the bridge, like wind over the hills

Everything we put our trust in has failed us, and we have failed each other

Age has become foolish; beauty is fleeting; strength is crippled now

Stricken we kneel before You, and all our works trail through our fingers like dust

Will the dust praise You? Will it tell of Your faithfulness?

O Lord, You have brought up my soul from Sheol; You restored me to life

Sing praises to the Lord, O you His saints, and give thanks to His holy Name

For His anger is but for a moment, and His favor is for a lifetime

Jesus Christ has bowed His head to the ground under the righteous anger of the Law

And from the dust He has been raised imperishable, that we might know God's favor

For such a great salvation I will praise You, Lord, for all time. Amen

~THURSDAY~

Lamentations 2:11 "My eyes are spent with weeping; my stomach churns; my bile is poured out to the ground because of the destruction of the daughter of my people, because infants and babies faint in the streets of the city."

It is all loss, Lord

It is all darkness

It is all sorrow

It is ruin

It is bitter separation

It is the agony of defeat, of utter destruction from within

What has come of all our hopes, but sadness? It is the fruits of sin:

Lies, hiding, murder, vengefulness, deceit, wrath, division, false doctrine, hatred, despair

And can any one of us say we did no wrong, said no wrong, thought no wrong?

No

Yet it is the young ones who suffer, and their eyes are wide with pain

From the shock of it they harden, and their paths are set in the same ways

What shall we say to them? For it was our devices, our waywardness that caused all this

Now therefore, O kings, be wise; be warned, O rulers of the earth

Serve the Lord with fear, and rejoice with trembling

Kiss the Son, lest He be angry, and you perish in the way

For His wrath is quickly kindled. Blessed are all who take refuge in Him. Amen

~FRIDAY~

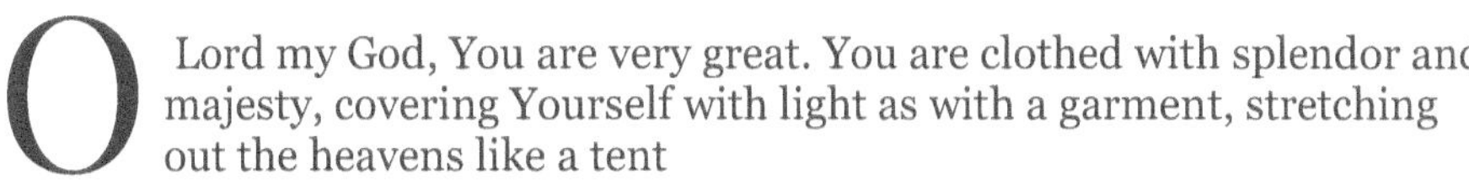

Lamentations 2:12 "They cry to their mothers, 'Where is bread and wine?' as they faint like a wounded man in the streets of the city, as their life is poured out on their mother's bosom."

O Lord my God, You are very great. You are clothed with splendor and majesty, covering Yourself with light as with a garment, stretching out the heavens like a tent

You make the clouds Your chariot; You ride on the wings of the wind. You make Your messengers winds; Your ministers a flaming fire

You cover the earth with the deep as with a garment; the waters stood above the mountains

You make springs gush forth in the valleys; they flow between the hills. They give drink to every beast of the field; the wild donkeys quench their thirst

Beside them the birds of the heavens dwell; they sing in the branches. From Your lofty abode You water the mountains; the earth is satisfied with the fruit of Your work

You cause the grass to grow for the livestock and plants for man to cultivate, that he may bring forth food from the earth and wine to gladden the heart of man, oil to make his face shine and bread to strengthen man's heart

The trees of the Lord are watered abundantly, the cedars of Lebanon He planted. He made the moon to mark the seasons; the sun knows its time for setting

The young lions roar for their prey, seeking their food from God. Man goes out to his work and to his labor until the evening

O Lord, how manifold are Your works! In wisdom have You made them all

These all look to You, to give them their food in due season. When You give it to them, they gather it up; when You hide Your face, they are dismayed

When You take away their breath, they die and return to the dust. May the glory of the Lord endure forever; may the Lord rejoice in His works

I will sing to the Lord as long as I live; I will sing praise to my God while I have being. Amen

~MONDAY~

Lamentations 2:13 "What can I say for you, to what compare you, O daughter of Jerusalem? What can I liken to you, that I may comfort you, O virgin daughter of Zion? For your ruin is vast as the sea; who can heal you?"

Lord, I have great sorrow and unceasing anguish in my heart

My conscience bears me witness in the Holy Spirit, for I could wish that I myself were accursed and cut off from Christ for the sake of my brothers

My kinsmen according to the flesh

Who are the Israelites. To them belong the adoption

The glory

The covenants

The giving of the Law

The worship

And the promises

To them belong the patriarchs, and from their race, according to the flesh, is the Christ, Who is God over all, blessed forever. Amen

But it is not as though the Word of God had failed. For not all who are descended from Israel belong to Israel

It is not the children of the flesh, but the children of the promise who are counted as offspring

So, brothers, we are not children of the slave woman, but of the free, and more are the offspring of the desolate one than of she who has a husband

When the fullness of time had come, God sent forth His Son, born of a woman, born under the Law, to redeem those who were under the Law

So that we might receive adoption as sons. And by His Spirit we cry, *"Abba, Father!"* Amen.

~TUESDAY~

Lamentations 2:14 "Your prophets have seen for you false and deceptive visions; they have not exposed your iniquity to restore your fortunes, but have seen for you oracles that are false and misleading."

What is prophecy, Lord? Is it not to utter dark sayings

To foretell what will come to pass

To speak words that are rich with wisdom

To look keenly down the corridors of time, and tell the people of God what will be

But without Your Spirit, all these things are a noisy gong, a clanging cymbal hanging before the temple of the false gods

From Aram Balak brought him, to curse Jacob and to denounce the people of Israel. For from the top of the crags he saw him:

"Behold, a people dwelling alone, and not counting themselves among the nations. God is not man, that He should lie; a son of man, that He should change His mind

For there shall be no enchantment against Jacob, no divination against Israel

Now it shall be said of Jacob and Israel, 'What hath God wrought!'"

The oracle of Balaam the son of Beor, of one whose eye saw clearly:

"I see Him, but not now; I behold Him, but not near. A star shall come out of Jacob, and a scepter shall rise out of Israel"

O my people, remember what Balak devised, and what Balaam son of Beor answered him, and what happened from Shittim to Gilgal, that you may remember the righteous acts of the Lord

When the people abandoned themselves to follow after the way of Balaam

And Phinehas son of Aaron brought a covenant of peace, by killing sin forever

The words of Him who has the sharp two-edged sword. Lord Jesus, we are yours alone. Amen

~WEDNESDAY~

Lamentations 2:15 "All who pass along the way clap their hands at you; they hiss and wag their heads at the daughter of Jerusalem: 'Is this the city that was called the perfection of beauty, the joy of all the earth?'"

She was Your city, Lord; You founded her. Your laws were the garland around her neck

Your Spirit called her out of the house of bondage; Your people took joy in her splendor

The old had comfort in her wide streets; the young ran and laughed through her flowing streams

Your holy mountain, beautiful in elevation: Mount Zion, in the far north, the city of the great King

And now, when the builders have laid the foundation of the temple of the Lord

The priests in their vestments came forward with trumpets and with cymbals to praise the Lord, according to the directions of David the king of Israel

And they sang responsively, praising and giving thanks to the Lord:

"For He is good, for His steadfast loves endures forever toward Israel"

And all the people shouted with a great shout when they praised the Lord, because the foundation of the house of the Lord was laid

But many of the priests and Levites and heads of fathers' houses, old men who had seen the first house, wept with a loud voice when they saw the foundation of the house being laid

So that the sound of joyful shout could not be distinguished from the people's weeping

Walk about Zion, go around her, number her towers, consider well her ramparts and citadels

That you may tell the next generation that this is God, our God forever and ever, and He will guide us forever. Amen

~THURSDAY~

Lamentations 2:16 "All your enemies rail against you; they hiss, they gnash their teeth, they cry: 'We have swallowed her! Ah, this is the day we longed for; now we have it; we see it!'"

Who is my enemy, Lord?

Is it that which would draw my heart away from You? Then it is the world

Who is my enemy? Is it that which boasts and is false to the truth? It is the flesh

Who is my enemy? Is it that which prowls around like a roaring lion, seeking to devour? It is the devil

How many years did we walk as enemies of the Cross of Christ

Our end was destruction, our god was our belly, and we gloried in our shame

With minds set on earthly things

With tears we confess it, Lord, and praise the day when, despite all our wars and strivings against You

Your Grace reached down and took us in, to make of such rebels citizens of Heaven, and more, to make us Your sons and daughters

From which we await a Savior, the Lord Jesus Christ

Who will transform our lowly body to be like His glorious Body

By the power that enables Him even to subject all things to Himself

Who then is the enemy, Lord? It is I

Who is my salvation? It is You, Lord

And You say to me, *"Love your enemies and pray for those who persecute you; for so I did for you."*

In this salvation, and in this alone, will I boast. It is all of grace. Amen, Lord Jesus, come quickly.

~FRIDAY~

Lamentations 2:17 "The Lord has done what he purposed; he has carried out his word, which he commanded long ago; he has thrown down without pity; he has made the enemy rejoice over you and exalted the might of your foes."

Yours, O Lord, is the greatness and the power and the glory and the victory and the majesty. For all that is in the heavens and in the earth is Yours

Yours is the kingdom, O Lord, and You are exalted as head above all. Both riches and honor come from You, and You rule over all

In Your hand are power and might, and in Your hand it is to make great and to give strength

You are God, and there is no other; You are God, and there is none like You, declaring the end from the beginning and from ancient times things not yet done

Saying, *"My counsel shall stand, and I will accomplish all my purpose."* You have established Your throne in the heavens, and Your kingdom rules over all

Do you not know? Have you not heard? Has it not been told you from the beginning? Have you not understood from the foundations of the earth?

It is He who sits above the circle of the earth, and its inhabitants are like grasshoppers

Who stretches out the heavens like a curtain, and spreads them like a tent to dwell in; Who brings princes to nothing, and makes the rulers of the earth as emptiness

In Him we have obtained an inheritance, having been predestined according to the purpose of Him who works all things according to the counsel of His will

So that we who were the first to hope in Christ might be to the praise of His glory: You who are the blessed and only Sovereign, the King of kings and Lord of lords

Who alone have immortality, Who dwell in unapproachable light, Whom no one has ever seen or can see. To You be honor and eternal dominion. Amen.

~MONDAY~

Lamentations 2:18 "Their heart cried to the Lord. O wall of the daughter of Zion, let tears stream down like a torrent day and night! Give yourself no rest, your eyes no respite!"

We are born to trouble, Lord, as the sparks fly upward

But You, O Lord–how long?

In death there is no remembrance of You. In Sheol, who will give You praise?

Turn, O Lord, deliver my life

Save me for the sake of Your steadfast love

What is the wall of the daughter of Zion?

Is it not the remnant of the Temple, the house built for Your glory?

These things I remember, as I pour out my soul

How I would go with the throng and lead them in procession to the house of God

With glad shouts and songs of praise

A multitude keeping festival

My soul is cast down within me; therefore I remember You

From the land of Jordan and of Hermon

From Mount Mizar

Deep calls to deep at the roar of Your waterfalls

All Your breakers and Your waves have gone over me

By day the Lord commands His steadfast love; at night His song is with me

Why are you cast down, O my soul, and why are you in turmoil within me?

Hope in God, for I shall again praise Him, my salvation and my God. Amen

~TUESDAY~

Lamentations 2:19 "Arise, cry out in the night, at the beginning of the night watches! Pour out your heart like water before the presence of the Lord! Lift your hands to him for the lives of your children, who faint for hunger at the head of every street."

In the night I have cried out to You, O Lord

May the Lord answer you in the day of trouble

I am surrounded by sorrow, overcome by grief; the chasms are too deep for me

May the Name of the God of Jacob protect you; may He send you help from the sanctuary

The heights are too far from me

And give you support from Zion

I have lost all the things that held my heart

May He remember all your offerings

And all the places that once were home to me are now barred away

And regard with favor your burnt sacrifices. Selah

Before You I pour out my heart, as its fondest hopes have vanished

May He grant you your heart's desire

In Your presence I lift my hands, as we faint for hunger

Now I know that the Lord saves His anointed

Who will come to save me? I have no hope but You, Lord

Some trust in chariots and some in horses

On You, Lord, and on You only, will I call. Hear my prayer. Amen.

But we trust in the name of the Lord our God.

~WEDNESDAY~

Lamentations 2:20 "Look, O Lord, and see! With whom have you dealt thus? Should women eat the fruit of their womb, the children of their tender care? Should priest and prophet be killed in the sanctuary of the Lord?"

Look at Your people, Lord

We are stricken

We fall before You

The dignity with which You created us is taken away

The enemy rejoices over our downfall

Truth is dragged through the streets

Your Name, which You placed upon us, is dishonored

Unspeakable things have been done among us

Our vision of what we love most about You–Your holiness–is obscured

What then is left? Has Your salvation been defeated?

For God alone, O my soul, wait in silence, for my hope is from Him

He only is my rock and my salvation, my fortress; I shall not be shaken

On God rests my salvation and my glory; my mighty rock, my refuge is God

Trust in Him at all times, O people; pour out your heart before Him

God is a refuge for us. *Selah*

Once God has spoken; twice I have heard this:

That power belongs to God

And that to You, O Lord, belongs steadfast love

Render to us according to the finished work of Jesus Christ today. Amen

~THURSDAY~

Lamentations 2:21 "In the dust of the streets lie the young and the old; my young women and my young men have fallen by the sword; you have killed them in the day of your anger, slaughtering without pity."

Is this the heart of God Almighty?

To slaughter indiscriminately, and leave the bodies of Your people to lie in the streets? To spend Your wrath on those who cannot save themselves?

All we can see is destruction. How can death be Your will?

But it is our foolish pride that has blinded us. For the door to Hell is locked from the inside

A great gulf is fixed between eternal life and eternal death, and there is but one bridge across it:

It is the Cross, the finished work of Jesus

It is His going under the waves for the last time, alone, to lift us up in the ark of Your mercy

It is His being lifted up on the tree of curse, that we might look on Him for blessing

It is the Landlord's Son sent to the vineyard to be slain by those He came to rescue

It is the full and free forgiveness of an atoning sacrifice for sin, once for all

Offered freely, yet requiring that we place ourselves in a place of complete dependence

And there is no other Way of deliverance; no other Name under Heaven given among men by which we must be saved

How shall we escape, if we neglect such a great salvation? This Jesus, the stone we have rejected: He has become the Cornerstone

This is the Lord's doing, and it is marvelous in our eyes. Come, Lord Jesus! Amen.

~FRIDAY~

Lamentations 2:22 "You summoned as if to a festival day my terrors on every side, and on the day of the anger of the Lord no one escaped or survived; those whom I held and raised my enemy destroyed."

Lord, You know my fears

The dark corners in the recesses of my memory

The accusations of the enemy that still echo in my mind

The betrayals that will forever wound my heart

The depths of terror where Your work in my soul was revealed

But You knew the way that I took

And You brought me forth tested as gold

For I know that my Redeemer lives

And at the last He will stand upon the earth

And after my skin has thus been destroyed

Yet in my flesh I shall see God

Whom I shall see for myself, and my eyes shall behold, and not another

On the Day of the anger of the Lord I shall escape

Come, my people, enter your chambers, and shut your doors behind you

Hide yourselves for a little while until the fury passes by

For behold, the Lord is coming out from His place to punish the inhabitants of the earth for their iniquity

Trust Him at all times, O people; pour out your heart before Him

God is a refuge for us. *Selah*

Amen

~MONDAY~

Lamentations 3:1 "I am the man who has seen affliction under the rod of his wrath"

I know my transgressions, Lord, and my sin is ever before me

Against You, You only, have I sinned, and done what is evil in Your sight

So that You may be justified in Your words and blameless in Your judgment

Behold, I was brought forth in iniquity, and in sin did my mother conceive me

And my heart struck me after what I had done

But now, O Lord, please take away the iniquity of Your servant, for I have done very foolishly

Three things the Lord offered me: *"Shall three years of famine come in the land?*

Or shall you flee three months before your foes while they pursue you?

Or shall there be three days' pestilence in the land?"

Then I said, *"I am in great distress. Let us fall into the hand of the Lord, for His mercy is great. But let me not fall into the hand of man"*

So the Lord sent a pestilence on His people from the morning until the appointed time

And when the angel stretched out his hand toward Jerusalem to destroy it, the Lord relented from the calamity, and said, *"It is enough; now stay your hand"*

I know now why You relented, Lord

It was because Your Son, Your only Son, took all our punishment, and loved us to the end

From His darkness we have light; by His wounds we have been healed. And in His resurrection is my great and only hope. Amen

~TUESDAY~

Lamentations 3:2 "He has driven and brought me into darkness without any light"

The Passover was coming, Lord, and the Son of Man was to be delivered and crucified

And at Bethany in the house of Simon the leper, a woman anointed Jesus' head with expensive perfume

The disciples were indignant, as it could have been given to the poor. But Jesus told them not to trouble her, for she had done a beautiful thing for Him

The poor we will always have with us, but we would not always have the Lord

In pouring the ointment on His body, she prepared Him for burial

Truly, He said to us, *wherever the Gospel is proclaimed in the whole world, what she did would also be told in memory of her*

At this, the son of perdition went out and betrayed Him. And reclining at the Passover table, Jesus prophesied what would happen to Him

That the Son of Man's time had come

That He would be betrayed and handed over to the Law

That He would die and be buried; that He would be driven and brought into a darkness that was without any light

That the Shepherd would be struck, and the sheep of the flock would be scattered

And offering us His very self, He said, *"Take, eat; this is My body"*

His blood to cover our sins, He said, *"This is the blood of the covenant. Drink of it, all of you"*

And the Sacrifice of such eternal worth was offered up and given to the poor; given for us; given for me

Lord Jesus, You are the Light of the world. Give us faith to follow You into eternal life. Amen

~WEDNESDAY~

Lamentations 3:3 "Surely against me he turns his hand again and again the whole day long."

It never seems to end, Lord. Trial after trial

Sorrow after sorrow

Loss after loss

All around us seem to be winning, and we must lose

They seem to have all they want in this life, with the approval of all around them

And we must be the scum of the earth, the refuse of all things

Yet it is not the loss of the world that grieves us; it is that Your hand seems to be turned against us

That our sin continues to grieve You; that our slowness of heart impedes our faith; that our failures must be forgiven again and again

Yet Your Spirit never falters. You never fail to show us the perfect finished work of Christ on our behalf

How the holy hand of the Law was turned against Him again and again, the whole day long

Until the day ended in a bitter and sightless night, without help or comfort

Yet even in the silent face of death, He rose in the power of an indestructible Life

And as surely as the Father raises the dead and gives them life, so also the Son gives life to whom He will

That whoever hears His Word and believes Him has eternal life. So we do not come into judgment, but have passed from death to life

Grant us to hear Your voice today, Lord Jesus, and may those who hear You live. Amen

~THURSDAY~

Lamentations 3:4 "He has made my flesh and my skin waste away; he has broken my bones"

The arrows of the Almighty are in me, Lord; my spirit drinks their poison

Is my strength the strength of stones, or is my flesh bronze? My days are swifter than a weaver's shuttle and come to their end without hope

What is man, that You make so much of him, and set Your heart on him?

Why do You not pardon my transgression and take away my iniquity?

Though I am in the right, I cannot answer You; I must appeal for mercy

For You are not a man, as I am, that I might answer You; that we should come to trial together

Does it seem good to You to oppress, to despise the work of Your hands and favor the designs of the wicked?

Have You eyes of flesh? Do You see as man sees?

Are Your days as the days of man, or Your years as a man's years? But I would speak to the Almighty, and argue my case with God:

That though He slay me, I will hope in Him.

For You have become a man, as I am, that You might answer me. Your spirit drank the poison of the Law's holy punishment

Your days came to their end without hope in this world

Your death pardoned my transgressions and took away my iniquity

Your eyes saw as man sees, and Your days were as the days of man

And You stand before the Almighty to argue my case with God. For I know that my Redeemer lives, and at the last He shall stand upon the earth

And after my skin has thus been destroyed, yet in my flesh I shall see God. Amen

~FRIDAY~

Lamentations 3:5 "He has besieged and enveloped me with bitterness and tribulation"

Bitterness is the opposite of sweetness, Lord. It is the knowledge of defeat

It is the shock of wrong triumphing over right, the horror of seeing the ones you love turn away from you

It is the salty taste of blood in the arena

It is the dark fog of war stealing over the peaceful countryside

It is the fruits of sin, the just deserts of forbidden love

It is the raw tearing away of innocence from beauty; it is the heart's cry at the last sword-stroke in the last battle of good and evil

And You know what it is to be enveloped with bitterness, Lord Jesus. For You knew defeat at the Cross

When wrong triumphed over You

When all men turned their faces from You, even Your own; when Your precious blood was spilt in our cause

When You stood against the rulers, the authorities, the cosmic powers, the spiritual forces of evil in the heavenly places

When You who knew no sin became sin, for us

When the only holy Son of God was cursed and hung on a tree

When You were the last warrior standing for God, and would not defend Yourself; and You fell

Yet the grave could not hold You down, and on the third day You rose again. Alleluia!

His mouth is most sweet, and He is altogether desirable. This is my Beloved and this is my Friend, O daughters of Jerusalem. Amen

~MONDAY~

Lamentations 3:6 "He has made me dwell in darkness like the dead of long ago."

We all have a past, Lord

It can be buried deep, long since remembered or shared:

Days we wish had never seen the light

Moments that never should have come about

Decisions we wish could be reversed

Places we never should have been

Desires that will not stand the test of Your holiness

Some part of us that had to die, that could not have come into the New Creation

Now the works of the flesh are evident: Sexual immorality, impurity, sensuality, idolatry, sorcery, enmity, strife, jealousy, fits of anger, rivalries, dissensions, divisions, envy, drunkenness, orgies, and the like

Such things will not inherit the Kingdom of God

But the fruit of the Spirit is love, joy, peace, patience, kindness, goodness, faithfulness, gentleness, self-control

Against such things there is no law

And those who belong to Christ have crucified the flesh with its passions and desires

Forgetting what lies behind, and straining forward to what lies ahead, I press on toward the goal for the prize of the upward call of God in Christ Jesus

Truly, truly, You said to us, an hour was coming, and is now here, when the dead will hear the voice of the Son of God, and those who hear will live

And we declare that You are the Son of God in power according to the Spirit of holiness by Your resurrection from the dead. Amen

~TUESDAY~

Lamentations 3:7 "He has walled me about so that I cannot escape; he has made my chains heavy"

It is a wall about us, this world we live in, this flesh we bear

Born to trouble as surely as the sparks fly upward; brought forth in iniquity and conceived in sin

For we know that the Law is spiritual. But I am of the flesh, sold under sin

So sin, seizing an opportunity through the commandment, deceived me and through it killed me

The Law is holy, and the commandment is holy and righteous and good. Did that which is good, then, bring death to me? By no means!

It was sin, producing death in me through what is good, so that sin might be shown to be sin

And through the commandment might become sinful beyond measure. I do not do what I want, but I do the very thing I hate

O wretched man that I am! Who will deliver me from this body of death?

Thanks be to God, through Jesus Christ our Lord

There is therefore now no condemnation for those who are in Christ Jesus

For the Law of the Spirit of life has set us free in Christ Jesus from the Law of sin and death; God has done what the Law, weakened by the flesh, could not do

By sending His own Son in the likeness of sinful flesh and for sin, He condemned sin in the flesh, in order that the righteous requirement of the Law might be fulfilled in us

Who walk not according to the flesh but according to the Spirit. And He who raised Christ Jesus from the dead will also give life to our mortal bodies

I would to God that all who hear me this day might become as I am, but for these chains. Amen

~WEDNESDAY~

Lamentations 3:8 "Though I call and cry for help, he shuts out my prayer"

I have cried out to You, Lord, but You have not answered

Your silence is never without cause

Search me, O God, and know my heart! Try me and know my thoughts. See if there be any grievous way in me, and lead me in the way everlasting:

If I have asked you with wrong motives, that I may spend it on my pleasures

If I have not shown honor to my wife and my prayers are hindered

If I have regarded wickedness in my heart, and the Lord does not hear me

If my hands are covered with blood, and when I have spread them out in prayer to You, You have hid Your eyes from me

If pride has risen in my heart and You have opposed me

If I have doubted in faith like a wave of the sea, driven and tossed by the wind, and will not receive anything from the Lord

If I have shut my ear to the cry of the poor, and will call out myself and not be answered

If I have hated good and loved evil, and torn the flesh from Your people, and You have hidden Your face from my evil deeds

As for You, O Lord, You will not restrain Your mercy from me; Your steadfast love and Your faithfulness will ever preserve me

For evils have encompassed me beyond number; my iniquities have overtaken me, and I cannot see. They are more than the hairs of my head; my heart fails me

But may all who seek You rejoice and be glad in You. May those who love Your salvation say continually, *"Great is the Lord!"*

As for me, I am poor and needy, but the Lord takes thought for me. You are my help and my deliverer; do not delay, O my God! Amen

~THURSDAY~

Lamentations 3:9 "He has blocked my ways with blocks of stones; he has made my paths crooked."

How can we know when we go astray, Lord?

Life is chaotic and disordered, a landscape thick with smoke we cannot see through

There are desires in our hearts that rise up, hopes and dreams that persist

Some of them are of You, and some of them are not

Cherished friends come and then they go

Some of them draw us nearer to You, and some of them drive a bitter wedge

Worldly goods appear, but moth and rust destroy, and thieves break in and steal

Wisdom attends us after battles hard won. But we grow forgetful, and do not remember her lessons

There are men and women of spiritual stature we look up to, giants in the faith

But they stumble and fall, some never to rise again; few there are that finish well

With the merciful You show Yourself merciful; with the blameless You show Yourself blameless

To the pure You show Yourself pure, but to the devious You show Yourself shrewd

You save the humble people but the haughty eyes You bring down

For it is You who light my lamp; the Lord God lightens my darkness

For by You I can run against a troop, and by my God I can leap over a wall

This God–His way is perfect; the Word of the Lord proves true. He is a shield for all those who take refuge in Him. Amen

~FRIDAY~

Lamentations 3:10 "He is a bear lying in wait for me, a lion in hiding"

Who is this God that I serve?

How can I describe Him

How can I tell the wonders I have seen

The works of His hands that are hidden from the world

The fear that grips my heart at His holiness

The miracles He has done in the world

The voice of the Lord over the waters

The God of glory thunders; the Lord, over many waters

The voice of the Lord is powerful, and full of majesty

The voice of the Lord breaks the cedars; the Lord breaks the cedars of Lebanon

He makes Lebanon to skip like a calf, and Sirion like a young wild ox

The voice of the Lord flashes forth flames of fire

The voice of the Lord shakes the wilderness

The Lord shakes the wilderness of Kadesh

The voice of the Lord makes the deer give birth, and strips the forests bare

And in His temple all cry, *"Glory!"*

The Lord sits enthroned over the flood

The Lord sits enthroned as King forever

May the Lord give strength to His people

May the Lord bless His people with peace. Amen

~MONDAY~

Lamentations 3:11 "He turned aside my steps and tore me to pieces; he has made me desolate"

Desolate places, Lord

It seems as if I see them wherever I go

Empty houses, yards strewn with belongings

Lost voices, people gone from their home

Deep loss, ragged gashes left in relationships

Mortal wounds

And over all of this there is always the eerie silence, like a torn blanket too heavy to lift

And I realize with a shock that all this is no window I see through, but a deadly mirror

When I come to pray, then, I cannot but do as the Saint from the City of God. I must begin by confessing my own desolation:

For I know that nothing good dwells in me, that is, in my flesh

And in that truth I move into my adoration:

One thing have I desired of the Lord, one thing will I seek after: That I may dwell in the house of the Lord, to behold the beauty of the Lord

Looking around at my fleshly desires, and seeing them to be as empty as the ruin of this world, I bring to You the only petition I have left:

Your Kingdom come, Your will be done, on earth as it is in Heaven

I lift to You, I commit to You my utter spiritual widowhood. I am lost and bereft without You

Visit me in my distress, and create in me by Your Spirit a religion that is pure and undefiled before You. Amen

~TUESDAY~

Lamentations 3:12 "He bent his bow and set me as a target for his arrow."

What are your arrows, Lord? Where are Your judgments?

How do You rule the earth? How is Your glory revealed?

Is this world not in the throes of death?

Then when sorrows and trials come, when they overwhelm us, we know they do but tell the truth

To follow Jesus, is that to prevail in the eyes of the world? We know it is not

For we are not greater than our Master

This is how one should regard us: As servants of Christ and stewards of the mysteries of God

Moreover, it is required of stewards that they be found faithful

But with me it is a very small thing that I should be judged by any human court

In fact, I do not even judge myself. For I am not aware of anything against myself, but I am not thereby acquitted

It is the Lord who judges me

Therefore do not pronounce judgment before the time, before the Lord comes

Who will bring to light the things now hidden in darkness and disclose the purposes of the heart; then each one will receive his commendation from God

If I am the target of Your arrow, Lord, I will trust unto death that it is for my life in Christ Jesus

For the Kingdom of God does not consist in talk, but in power

Hallelujah! Salvation and glory and power belong to our God. Blessed be Your Name. Amen

~WEDNESDAY~

Lamentations 3:13 "He drove into my kidneys the arrow of his quiver"

It feels as though all this has gone to my heart, Lord

I have given my utmost for Your Kingdom; I have offered my most sincere work

I have dedicated my time and resources; I have given freely, with no thought of return

I have persevered long after hope grew dim; I have spoken Your Word to the ignorant

I have wept with the hurting

I have rejoiced with the triumphant

I have spoken truth to power, and been crushed for it

I have left houses and brothers and sisters and father and mother and children and fields for Your sake

I have accepted ruin and loss and ill repute and rebuke and suspicion

And for what? Life goes on, and little is the difference the world can see for it all

It is not enough; I am not enough

Yet I raise my eyes, and by faith I see Your Kingdom coming, slowly but surely: I see Your Church arising, terrible as an army with banners

I see Your judgment on the wicked man, and Your commendation on the righteous

I could not give people what they needed most. But it is well with my soul

For I have been crucified with Christ. It is no longer I who live, but Christ who lives in me

And the life I now live in the flesh I live by faith in the Son of God, who loved me and gave himself for me. Amen

~THURSDAY~

Lamentations 3:14 "I have become the laughingstock of all peoples, the object of their taunts all day long."

There is a way of the world, Lord, a way to make your way in it

To find your place in the world, or rather to let it find its place in you

To curry favor with those who keep the gates of access; to make yourself look good to all who are watching

To achieve the inner circle, that nebulous and elusive relational core we spend so much of our lives seeking

To convince all around you that you are one of them, that you "get it," that you are not "that guy"

To be privy to the things spoken in hushed tones not meant for the ears of the great unwashed

To know that there is a seat in the halls of power with your name on it; that you have a place in the smoke-filled room

And it is all utter and disastrous madness, a chasing after the wind, nothing but pride codified

The kings of the earth set themselves, and the rulers take counsel together

Against the Lord and against His Anointed, saying, *"Let us burst their bonds apart, and cast away their cords from us"*

He who sits in the heavens laughs; the Lord holds them in derision. Then He will speak to them in His wrath, and terrify them in His fury, saying: *"As for Me, I have set My King on Zion, My holy hill"*

For the Lord sees not as man sees. Man looks on the outward appearance, but the Lord looks on the heart

I will gladly be a fool in the eyes of the world, if that is the cost of faithful witness to Jesus Christ my Lord, for whose sake I have suffered the loss of all things

Blessed are all who take refuge in Him. Amen

~FRIDAY~

Lamentations 3:15 "He has filled me with bitterness; he has sated me with wormwood.

This world is no friend to grace

We live in it, but we are not of it, Lord

When good things come, we joy in them, and we give You thanks; they fade away, as all good things do, save You only

And we watch them go

We do not mourn them, for our life is not in them

We lift holy hands together, and we say:

The Lord gives, and the Lord has taken away

Blessed be the Name of the Lord

Blessed be the Name of the Lord from this time forth and forevermore

From the rising of the sun to its setting, the Name of the Lord is to be praised

Who is like the Lord our God, who is seated on high

Who looks far down on the heavens and the earth?

He raises the poor from the dust and lifts the needy from the ash heap

Do not call me Naomi; call me Mara, for the Almighty has dealt very bitterly with me

I went away full, and the Lord has brought me back empty

Trust in Him at all times, O people; pour out your heart before Him

God is a refuge for us. *Selah*

On God rests my salvation and my glory; my mighty Rock, my Refuge is God. Amen

~MONDAY~

Lamentations 3:16 "He has made my teeth grind on gravel, and made me cower in ashes"

We want to live, Lord; we hold onto life dearly

The days in the sun linger in our memories

We greet our brothers and love those who love us

Enemies are avoided, and those who have threatened us we keep at arm's length

We cling to hopes and dreams; we build new barns and storehouses for our wealth

We heap up our treasure in this world, and feast our eyes on it

But Your Word tells us that are these vain pursuits are death, not life. You said that whoever would save his life, must lose it

You said that if in this life only we have hope, we are of all men most to be pitied

You said that even the Gentiles love those who love in return

You said to love our enemies, and do good to those who persecute us

You said to take up our cross and follow You, if we would be Your disciple

You said, *"You fool! This very night your life will be required of you"*

You told us to store up treasures in Heaven, where our heart would be also

We want to live forever, Lord, with You

And those who speak thus make it clear that they are seeking a homeland

We desire a better country; a Heavenly one

Therefore You are not ashamed to be called our God, for You have prepared for us a City. Amen

~TUESDAY~

Lamentations 3:17 "My soul is bereft of peace; I have forgotten what happiness is"

Long have I searched for what my soul desires, Lord

I have looked for it in achievement

In difficult toil

In friendship

In shared experience

In community

In learning and knowledge

In beauty

In thought and reflection

In laughter and tears

But all of it came to an end; all of it failed

"Peace, peace," they said, but there was no peace

And never would be, until I came into Your presence. Until I came to worship

Then I saw what Jesus Christ has done for me

And I knew that it was a truth my soul could rest on

Solid joys and lasting treasures, none but Zion's children know

Let me keep my eyes fixed on Your Cross, Lord; let me see Your glory

Glory as of the only Son from the Father, full of grace and truth

And from Your fullness I have received, grace upon grace

Amen

~WEDNESDAY~

Lamentations 3:18 "So I say, 'My endurance has perished; so has my hope from the Lord.'"

I am only a man, Lord

This is just flesh

I cannot contend in the heavens with my enemies

When the battle rages, I am wounded

When the road stretches through the desert, I thirst

When friendships are severed, I mourn; when Your Word is maligned, I am angry

But my anger does not bring about the righteousness of God

The days of my life are spent, they are rolled up like a scroll before me

In my heart are the highways to Zion; but the way is long, and my flesh rebels

God shall arise, His enemies shall be scattered, and those who hate Him shall flee before Him

As smoke is driven away, so You shall drive them away; as wax melts before fire, so the wicked shall perish before God

Father of the fatherless and protector of widows is God in His holy habitation

The earth quaked, the heavens poured down rain

Before God, the One of Sinai

Before God, the One of Israel

You ascended on high, leading captives in Your train, and giving gifts to men

Even among the rebellious, that the Lord God may dwell there

Dwell in my heart today, by the power and grace of the Cross of Christ. Amen

~THURSDAY~

Lamentations 3:19 "Remember my affliction and my wanderings, the wormwood and the gall!"

For every dream that has been lost, Lord; for every time the world has called me a fool

For every friend who has turned their back; for every ambition I have set aside

For every treasure of Egypt I have traded for the reproach of Christ; for every sidelong look I have received for following You

For every time I have been passed over for being faithful; for every time my Gospel has been condemned as fundamentalism

For every time my reverence of Your Name has been received with mocking; for every time my faithfulness is returned with malice

For every deep truth that is repaid with shallow falsehood

I gather up all these things and I look at them, and my heart is swept with sadness

You have called me to be in this world, but not of it; did You really call me to this?

And I remember the Man of Sorrows, Jesus Christ my Lord; and I know that You did. He was despised and rejected of men, a man of sorrows and acquainted with grief

As one from whom men hide their faces, He was despised, and we esteemed Him not

O Jerusalem, Jerusalem, the city that kills the prophets and stones those who are sent to it! How often would I have gathered your children together as a hen gathers her brood under her wings, and you were not willing!

And as I slowly begin to see this broken world through Your eyes, I do not lose heart. For this light momentary affliction is preparing for me an eternal weight of glory beyond all comparison

As I look to the things that are unseen, to the Eternal. I look to You, Lord. Amen

~FRIDAY~

Lamentations 3:20 "My soul continually remembers it and is bowed down within me."

Some things I can never forget, Lord; some wounds that will never be healed in this life

Some dark scenes that will always haunt my memory; some struggles that can never be forgotten

Healing that will not be fully realized until I look You in the face

A pain that goes far beyond any physical reaction or consequence; a deep, abiding, gnawing, searing anguish

The knowledge that people I will always love have turned away from life forever

That Death has triumphed over them at last

The nations have defiled Your holy temple; that they have laid Jerusalem in ruins

They have given the bodies of Your servants to the birds of the heavens for food, the flesh of Your faithful to the beasts of the earth

They have poured out their blood like water all around Jerusalem, and there was none to bury them

How long, O Lord? Will You be angry forever?

You took from the hand of the Lord the cup of the wine of His wrath, and You drained it to its dregs

Death triumphed over You; Your body was hung on the cursed tree; Your blood was poured out like water; there was none to rescue You

Lord Jesus, You have taken on all the sin and curse and sadness of the world, for Your elect

But we Your people, the sheep of Your pasture, find in You our only comfort

Let me hear in the morning of Your steadfast love. Amen

~MONDAY~

Lamentations 3:21 "But this I call to mind, and therefore I have hope"

Lord, we are but flesh; the waves batter against us

The wind lashes at us in its fury, the bitter cold seizes our hearts

How can we stand in such a storm?

I said, *"Let me remember my song in the night; let me meditate in my heart*

Will the Lord spurn forever? Has His steadfast love forever ceased?"

Then I said, *"I will appeal to this, to the years of the right hand of the Most High"*

I will remember the deeds of the Lord; yes, I will remember Your wonders of old

I will ponder all Your work, and meditate on Your mighty deeds

Your way, O God, is holy. What god is great like our God?

You are the God who works wonders; You have made known Your might among the peoples

You with Your arm redeemed Your people, the children of Jacob and Joseph. *Selah*

When the waters saw You, O God

When the waters saw You, they were afraid; indeed, the deep trembled

The crash of Your thunder was in the whirlwind; Your lightnings lighted up the world

Your way was through the sea, Your path through the great waters; yet Your footprints were unseen

You led Your people like a flock, by the hand of Moses and Aaron

Our hope is in You, Lord. Amen

~TUESDAY~

Lamentations 3:22 "The steadfast love of the Lord never ceases; his mercies never come to an end"

We rush through this world together, Lord

Seeking, always seeking. Trying to find something we have lost

Trying to right something we have gotten terribly wrong

Trying to fill something that is empty

Trying to mend something that is hopelessly torn; trying to see what has been hidden all our lives

And when all these vain pursuits have ended in failure, we turn on each other in anger and fear, trying to hide our distress in ferocity

Dead in trespasses and sins, sons of disobedience, by nature children of wrath

Here You found us, and here You could have left us, and none would have gainsaid

But God, being rich in mercy, because of the great love with which You loved us, even when we were dead in our trespasses

Made us alive together with Christ – By grace we have been saved – raised us up and seated us with Him in the heavenly places in Christ Jesus

So that in the coming ages You might show the immeasurable riches of Your grace in kindness toward us in Christ Jesus

For by grace we have been saved through faith. And this is not our own doing; it is the gift of God, not a result of works, that no one may boast

We are Your workmanship, Lord. Speak Your love and mercy to a dying world through us

To make known among the Gentiles this ceaseless Gospel of salvation by grace through faith:

Christ in us, the hope of glory. Amen

~WEDNESDAY~

Lamentations 3:23 "They are new every morning; great is your faithfulness."

Once again, Lord, I have fallen short

Incline Your ear, O Lord, and answer me, for I am poor and needy

Once again I have brushed against Death, and my heart has quailed before it

Preserve my life, for I am godly

Once again I have forgotten Your holy Law; once again I have been swept up in the foolish hopes of this world

Gladden the soul of Your servant, for to You, O Lord, do I lift up my soul; for You, O Lord, are good and forgiving

Once again the strength of my arm is not enough to deliver; once again I have trusted in my own wisdom, my own salvation, my own works

In the day of my trouble I call upon You, for You answer me; there is none like You among the gods, O Lord, nor are there any works like Yours

Once again I will humble myself, and call on You alone for rescue; once again I will proclaim Your goodness in the assembly of the righteous

For You are great and do wondrous things; You alone are God; teach me Your way, O Lord, that I may walk in Your truth

Once again I will lift high the blessed Cross of Christ before a dying world

I give thanks to You, O Lord my God, with my whole heart, and I will glorify Your Name forever

Once again I will follow You in the joy of new life and redemption, wherever Your Spirit leads

For great is Your steadfast love toward me; You have delivered my soul from the depths of Sheol

Great is Thy faithfulness, Lord, unto me. Amen.

~THURSDAY~

Lamentations 3:24 "The Lord is my portion," says my soul, "therefore I will hope in him."

The sons of Levi had no portion, Lord. All their brothers were given land divided by lot

According to the names of the tribes of their fathers they inherited it; according to the number of names the land was divided for inheritance

Even the daughters of Zelophehad, for their bold faith, were rewarded by the Lord with an inheritance

But the Levites were given the firstfruits of the grain, of the wine and oil, and the first fleece of the sheep

And they had no portion or inheritance with Israel; but the Lord was their inheritance, as You promised them

And in this way we walk also, close to the way of the Cross

Being built up as a spiritual house, to be a holy priesthood, to offer spiritual sacrifices acceptable to God through Jesus Christ

The appointed time has grown very short. From now on, let those who have wives live as though they had none; and those who mourn as if they were not mourning

And those who rejoice as though they were not rejoicing; and those who buy as though they had no goods; and those who deal with the world as though they had no dealings with it

For the present form of this world is passing away

And the One of whom these things were spoken belonged to another tribe, from which no one has ever served at the altar, to whom Levi himself, who receives tithes, paid tithes through his ancestor Abraham

He has become a priest not on the basis of a legal requirement concerning bodily descent, but by the power of an indestructible life

The kingdoms of this world are become the Kingdoms of our Lord, and of His Christ! Amen.

~FRIDAY~

Lamentations 3:25 "The Lord is good to the one who waits for him, to the soul who seeks him."

This is the hardest thing, Lord. Noah waited a hundred years, while he obeyed Your Word

Job, in all his sorrow and loss, said, *"All the days of my service I would wait"*

Abraham waited twenty-five years till his son was born, the child of promise

Joseph was unjustly put in slavery and in prison as he waited for Your rescue

Forty years Moses tended sheep in the desert, and forty more he led Israel

Hannah did not care what others thought, till she received the Lord's promise

Ruth would not leave Naomi, but said, *"Where you go I will go"* as she waited for her kinsman-redeemer

Esther knew she had been raised up for just such a time of deliverance

David submitted to Saul's ungodly rule for years until he was given the throne

Jeremiah spoke these very words we meditate on: *"The Lord is good to the one who waits for Him, to the soul who seeks Him"*

The prophetess Anna did not depart from the Temple as she worshiped with fasting and prayer night and day, until she saw the Messiah in her day

Simeon waited for the consolation of Israel, and the Spirit revealed to him that he would not see death before he had seen the Lord's Christ

When Jesus Christ came in the flesh–Immanuel, God with us–He said, *"The time is fulfilled, and the Kingdom of God is at hand. Repent, and believe the Gospel"*

For when the fullness of time had come, God sent forth his Son, born of woman under the law, to redeem those who were under the law, so that we might receive adoption as sons

It is for You, Jesus, that we wait; for You alone. Come quickly, Lord. Amen.

~MONDAY~

Lamentations 3:26 "It is good that one should wait quietly for the salvation of the Lord."

To hear the promises of Your Covenant, Lord

To face their staggering unreality square on

These guarantees that we and our offspring will be heirs of the world, just as Abraham was

Not to suppose that adherents of the Law will be the heirs, for then faith would be null and the promise void

For to the one who works, his wages are not counted as a gift but as his due. And to the one who does not work but believes in Him who justifies the ungodly, his faith is counted as righteousness

Just as David speaks of the blessing of the one to whom God counts righteousness apart from works:

"Blessed are those whose lawless deeds are forgiven, and whose sins are covered; blessed is the man against whom the Lord will not count his sin"

For the Law brings wrath, but where there is no Law there is no transgression. That is why it depends on faith, in order that the promise may rest on grace and be guaranteed to all his offspring

To the one who shares the faith of Abraham, who is the father of us all

To the one who receives the mighty promises of the Covenant: The Son, the Land, the Nation, and the Blessing

In hope our father believed against hope, that he should become the father of many nations

Lord of hosts, let no unbelief make us waver concerning Your promise

But let us grow strong in our faith as we give glory to God, fully convinced that You are able to do what You promised

And count this faith to us as righteousness, for Christ's sake. Amen

~TUESDAY~

Lamentations 3:27 "It is good for a man that he bear the yoke in his youth."

The yokes that You have laid on me, Lord

They have been heavy, and they have been grievous, that yoke of servitude to harsh masters:

Masters such as achievement, approval, distinguishment, attainment, acclaim, importance

That crushing, bitter yoke of false desire. Only Your Spirit can ever know how deeply it was seated

How unwilling I was that it should ever be lifted away; how long I continued along its unshakeable track

How fiercely I rankled that the sway it held over me should ever have been discovered

How long I opposed the Voice that kept pursuing me, that called me, long after any other would have ceased to care:

"Come to Me, all you who labor and are heavy laden, and I will give you rest

Take My yoke upon you, and learn of Me, for I am gentle and lowly of heart

And you will find rest for your soul.

For My yoke is easy, and My burden is light."

And in sudden anguished birth of joy I came out into the Light

Only to discover that it was the Light that had come into me, after all

And this light momentary affliction was preparing for me a weight of glory beyond all comparison

As I look not to the things that are seen, but to the One who is unseen

Lord Jesus, be glorified in me today, and receive me into glory. Amen

~WEDNESDAY~

Lamentations 3:28 "Let him sit alone in silence when it is laid on him"

There are some truths that cannot be spoken with words, Lord, some knowledge that ought not to be distilled into speech

Some experiences that would not be dignified with sharing

Some realizations that are too shattering to be said

Some sorrow that must be kept in silence, until it all brims over in Your presence:

Betrayals that run deep

Evil that is almost innocent in its contrived aspect

Lies that sweep through the hearts of the faithful, turning their eyes blind

Vicious attacks on Your people that wound and divide

Cruel rewards for truth-telling that lay on heavy burdens, but will not lift a finger to move them

Therefore he who is prudent will keep silent in such a time, for it is an evil time

Woe to you who desire the Day of the Lord! Why would you have the Day of the Lord? Is not the Day of the Lord darkness, and not light, and gloom with no brightness in it?

Seek good, and not evil, that you may live. Seek the Lord and live, lest He break out like fire in the house of Joseph

But when He was accused by the chief priests and elders, He gave no answer

And Pilate said, *"Do you not hear how many things they testify against You?"* But He gave them no answer, not even to a single charge. Like a sheep that before its shearers is silent, so He opened not His mouth

Yet He bore the sin of many, as intercession for the transgressors; for me

This truth I will speak, and shout it with the multitude: Jesus is Lord! Amen.

~THURSDAY~

Lamentations 3:29 "Let him put his mouth in the dust– there may yet be hope"

We are dust, Lord, and to dust we shall return

You formed us from the dust of the earth, put Your breath in us, proclaimed us good

Made in Your image, a little lower than the heavenly beings, crowned with glory and honor

Bless the Lord, O my soul, and forget not all His benefits, who forgives all your iniquity; who heals all your diseases; who redeems your life from the pit

Who crowns you with steadfast love and mercy; who satisfies you with good, so that your youth is renewed like the eagle's

The Lord works righteousness and justice for all who are oppressed. The Lord is merciful and gracious, slow to anger and abounding in steadfast love

He does not deal with us according to our sins, nor repay us according to our iniquities. For as high as the heavens are above the earth, so great is His steadfast love toward those who fear Him

For He knows our frame; He remembers that we are dust

And we have this mind in ourselves, which is ours in Christ Jesus:

Who though He was in the form of God, did not count equality with God a thing to be grasped, but emptied Himself, by taking the form of a servant, being born in the likeness of men

And being found in human form, He humbled Himself by becoming obedient to the point of death, even death on a Cross

Therefore God has highly exalted Him and bestowed on Him the Name that is above every name, so that at the Name of Jesus every knee should bow

And every tongue confess that Jesus Christ is Lord. Bless the Lord, O my soul

Amen

~FRIDAY~

Lamentations 3:30 "Let him give his cheek to the one who strikes, and let him be filled with insults."

Who would reject the Messiah of Israel?

Who would kill the Son of the Master of the house?

Who has been partners in the blood of the prophets?

What did we go out in the wilderness to see:

A reed shaken by the wind? A man dressed in soft clothing?

Behold, those who wear soft clothing are in kings' houses

What then did we go out to see: A prophet?

Yes, I tell you, and more than a prophet

This is he of whom it is written:

Behold, I send My messenger before your face, who will prepare your way before you

John baptized us with water for repentance, but He who came after John is mightier than he, whose sandals none are worthy to carry

He will baptize us with the Holy Spirit and with fire; His winnowing fork is in His hand, and He will clear His threshing floor and gather His wheat into His barn

But the chaff He will burn with unquenchable fire

Who would reject the Messiah of Israel? It was I, Lord

I rejected Him; I struck His cheek; I filled Him with insults

And He stretched out His arms, and cried, *"Father, forgive them, for they know not what they do"*

I have been forgiven much; Lord, let me love much. Blessed be Your Name. Amen

~MONDAY~

Lamentations 3:31 "For the Lord will not cast off forever"

This, Lord–

This.

We know why You have cast off; we know why Your judgment has come

Why the enemy has prevailed over us

Why the years of joy and plenty are gone forever

Why the friends we loved more than our own selves have turned away

Why the good things stored up for many years are vanished

Why the hopes and dreams we lived for have faded; why the laughter that used to ring in our halls has turned to tears

It is because we have lost our first love; we have turned our backs on You

And in love Jesus Christ took all of our judgment on Himself

The enemy rejoiced over Him when He fell; He knew want and emptiness

His friend greeted Him with a traitor's kiss, and all the others ran away

He did not have a place to lay His head; His Father turned His face away in the hour of darkness

Behold, and see if there be any sorrow like His sorrow

For the hour has come for the Son of Man to be glorified

Truly, truly I say unto you, unless a grain of wheat falls into the earth and dies, it remains alone

But if it dies, it bears much fruit. And You have not cast off forever

We love not our lives unto death, Lord, and we would follow You to eternal life. Amen

~TUESDAY~

Lamentations 3:32 "But, though he cause grief, he will have compassion according to the abundance of his steadfast love"

Lord, You see all; You know all. You have all things in the palm of Your hand

Behold, the nations are as a drop in a bucket; they are accounted as dust on the scales

Behold, You take up the coastlands like fine dust

Do you not know? Have you not heard? Has it not been told you from the beginning? Have you not understood from the foundations of the earth?

It is He who sits above the circle of the earth, and all its inhabitants are like grasshoppers

Who stretches out the heavens like a curtain, and spreads them like a tent to dwell in

Who brings princes to nothing, and makes the rulers of the earth as emptiness

"To whom then will you compare Me, that I should be like him?" says the Holy One. Lift up your eyes on high and see who created these

He who brings out their host by number, calling them all by name

By the greatness of His might, and because He is strong in power, not one is missing

Why do you say, O Jacob, and speak, O Israel: *"My way is hidden from the Lord, and my right is disregarded by my God"*

The Lord is the everlasting God, the Creator of the ends of the earth

They who wait for the Lord shall renew their strength; they shall mount up with wings like eagles. They shall run and not be weary; they shall walk and not faint

Lord Jesus, You are my great hope in grief and sorrow. Have compassion on me today. Amen.

~WEDNESDAY~

Lamentations 3:33 "For he does not afflict from his heart or grieve the children of men."

They have finished their work, Lord; They have utterly betrayed and abandoned

What once was trust is now shattered, never to be put together again

What once was love is now estrangement

What once was brotherly and sisterly love is now astonished grief

What once was solid truth is now smooth manipulation

What once was the bond of unity is now hostility

What once was sweet fellowship is now posturing and hiding. And in the wreckage of all this, our spirits are drawn to remember

That if we had not elevated each other to idolatry, this would never have happened

So we return to You once again, to the God who bought us with Your own Son

Behold, as the eyes of servants look to the hand of their master, as the eyes of a maidservant to the hand of her mistress

So our eyes look to the Lord our God, till He has mercy on us

Have mercy upon us, have mercy upon us. For we have had more than enough of contempt

Our soul has had more than enough of the scorn of those who are at ease, of the contempt of the proud

For God opposes the proud, but gives grace to the humble

By the meekness and gentleness of Christ, we beseech You: Destroy every argument and every lofty opinion raised against the knowledge of God

And gather us into the everlasting arms. Amen.

~THURSDAY~

Lamentations 3:34 "To crush underfoot all the prisoners of the earth"

We know what it feels like, Lord, to be crushed underfoot

To know total defeat; to watch your friends move away

To watch your enemies rejoice over you

To remember that you could have avoided this by abandoning your principles

To watch the world with all its pleasures fade away

To settle in to the long punishment of isolation; to see your hopes and dreams disappear

And to seek the face of the Lord, when all else has failed

The Lord is my portion; I promise to keep all Your words

I entreat Your favor with all my heart; be gracious to me according to Your promise

When I think on my ways, I turn my feet to Your testimonies; I hasten and do not delay to keep Your commandments

Though the cords of the wicked ensnare me, I do not forget Your Law

At midnight I rise to praise You, because of Your righteous rules

The Lord is on my side; I will not fear. What can man do to me?

The Lord is on my side as my helper; I shall look in triumph on those who hate me

It is better to take refuge in the Lord than to trust in man; it is better to take refuge in the Lord than to trust in princes

I shall not die, but I shall live, and recount the deeds of the Lord

Show me Your salvation today, Lord

Amen

~FRIDAY~

Lamentations 3:35 "to deny a man justice in the presence of the Most High"

You see all things, Lord; You see when brother murders brother

You see when the intention of the thoughts of man's heart are only evil all the time

When people are mistreated and sent away

When perversion arises and men are inflamed with lust

When the love of the world sweeps someone into destruction

When unlawful consanguinity is entered into

When brother deceives brother

When father-in-law defrauds son-in-law

When innocence is violated

When brutal revenge is taken

When brother envies brother; when malice separates families

When father-in-law commits evil against daughter-in-law

When purity is repaid with vengeance

When the long, slow arm of justice finally catches up with guilt

And the older brother says, *"Take my life, instead of his."* And in this beautiful picture, faded and marred though it is, we see His face who gave His life for ours

He who knew no sin was made to be sin, that we might become the righteousness of God

Lord Jesus, You are our Rock; Your work is perfect, for all Your ways are justice. Amen

~MONDAY~

Lamentations 3:36 "to subvert a man in his lawsuit, the Lord does not approve."

The Law is holy, Lord, and the commandment is holy and righteous and good

It is we who are evil

It is we who try to defraud each other

It is we who bite and devour

It is we who do harm to one another

It is we who did not know what it was to covet, until the Law said, *"Do not covet"*

And sin seizing an opportunity through the commandment, produced in me all kinds of covetousness

I was once alive apart from the Law, but when the commandment came, sin came alive and I died

The very commandment that promised life proved to be death to me. Did that which is good, then, bring death to me? By no means!

It was sin, producing death in me through what is good

In order that sin might be shown to be sin

And through the commandment might become sinful beyond measure. For we know that the Law is spiritual, but I am of the flesh, sold under sin

For I do not do what I want, but I do the very thing I hate

Wretched man that I am! Who will rescue me from this body of death? Thanks be to God, through Jesus Christ our Lord

So Love is the fulfillment of the Law

And greater love has no one than Jesus Christ, who laid down His life for me. Amen.

~TUESDAY~

Lamentations 3:37 "Who has spoken and it came to pass, unless the Lord has commanded it?"

Not my words, Lord

Not my vision

Not my pronouncement

Not my faithfulness

Not my blessing

Not my curse

Not my power, not my glory, but Yours

Not to us, O Lord, not to us

But to Your name give glory

For the sake of Your steadfast love and Your faithfulness

Why should the nations say, *"Where is their God?"*

Our God is in the heavens; He does all that He pleases

Their idols are silver and gold, the work of human hands

They have mouths, but do not speak; eyes, but do not see; ears, but do not hear

Those who make them become like them; so do all who trust in them

O Israel, trust in the Lord! He is their help and their shield

O house of Aaron, trust in the Lord! He is their help and their shield

You who fear the Lord, trust in the Lord! He is our help and our shield

But we will bless the Lord from this time forth and forevermore. Praise the Lord! Amen.

~WEDNESDAY~

Lamentations 3:38 "Is it not from the mouth of the Most High that good and bad come?"

It is a fearsome thing to be in Your presence, Lord

To know that all that is good derives its being from You

To know that all things are in Your hand

To know that all will give an account to You for our words and deeds

To see that judgment will surely be given in the end

That the plans of the wicked will founder, and the hope of the righteous will be well placed

That the grievous trials we faced in this life will be turned in Your hand so that all can see

That their light momentary affliction produces in us a weight of glory beyond all comparison, as we look not to the things that are seen but to the things that are unseen

For the things that are seen are transient, but the things that are unseen are eternal

Since we have the same spirit of faith according to what has been written: *"I believed, and so I spoke"*

We also believe, and so we also speak. For God, who said *"Let light shine out of darkness"* has shone in our hearts

To give the light of the knowledge of the glory of God in the face of Jesus Christ

For I am not ashamed of the Gospel, for it is the power of God for salvation to everyone who believes, to the Jew first and also to the Greek

For in it the righteousness of God is revealed from faith to faith. As it is written, *"The righteous shall live by faith"*

By every Word that proceeds from Your mouth, Lord. Amen

~THURSDAY~

Lamentations 3:39 "Why should a living man complain, a man, about the punishment of his sins?"

It is all around us, Lord: Wrongdoing, untruth, cruelty, harm

The fruits of our first parents' decision to disobey You

To take on themselves the burden of determining right from wrong

To set at naught Your warning: *"In the day that you eat of it you shall surely die"*

To abdicate their posts as stewards over Creation

To sit on the throne of God Himself as judges of good and evil

And then to cast their eye on the Tree of Life and eat of it too, and live in death forever

But You went looking for them in the Garden. You confronted them with their sin, and named it, and condemned it

Not named as the works of God were, the lights of the heavens and the creatures of the earth, but named as an evil that You had not spoken into existence in the dawn of Time

And You set your Law as a flaming sword between them and the beauty they had known; curse and exile would be their path until their last breath

Yet even in judgment, Your heart was for mercy and grace. *"He shall crush your head, and you shall bruise His heel,"* You said to the serpent

And all the envy, murder, strife, deceit, and maliciousness of the world fell on Your shoulders

As Moses lifted up the serpent in the wilderness, so the Son of Man was lifted up, that whoever believes in Him should not perish, but have eternal life

Let us turn away from our sin, and cast it at the foot of the Cross, and bear it no more

And setting our eyes on You, walk before You in holiness forever. Amen

~FRIDAY~

Lamentations 3:40 "Let us test and examine our ways, and return to the Lord!"

Lord, who has even begun to know his own heart, that he could examine it

For I know that my heart is innately twisted in on itself. I would seek my own glory

I would not have the Lord to rule over me, but I would be God myself

I would not offer true worship in Spirit and in truth

I would have those things which belong to others

I would shirk my own duties You have given me

I would shift the blame of my sin onto others. For all this I would have all men think well of me

And I would sacrifice all the world to my own foolish desires, wishes, dreams

Therefore you have no excuse, O man, every one of you who judges. For in passing judgment on another you condemn yourself, because you, the judge, practice the very same things

Do you suppose, O man, that you will escape the judgment of God? Or do you presume on the riches of His kindness and forbearance and patience, not knowing that God's kindness is meant to lead you to repentance?

But because of our hard and impenitent hearts we are storing up wrath for ourselves on the Day of Wrath, when God's righteous judgment will be revealed

What does it mean, then, to test and examine our ways? To put my faith, fully and completely, in this:

That You will render to each one according to his works: To those who by patience in well-doing seek for glory and honor and immortality, You will give eternal life

And because of the finished work of Jesus Christ alone, I am found righteous in Him. Amen

~MONDAY~

Lamentations 3:41 "Let us lift up our hearts and hands to God in heaven"

You are holy, Lord; You are good. You are righteous, just, and true

You speak, and it comes to pass. You act, and the mountains crumble before You

You perform Your will, and the wind and the waves obey; Your ways are beyond knowing, Your works beyond mastering

In Heaven is Your throne, and lifted high above all things Your holy habitation; yet in mercy You remember the lowly and the downtrodden

Your grace is the boast of the widow and the fatherless; Your compassion is the hope of those who cannot keep themselves alive

Who is like our Lord? Who has commanded the dawn, or stretched out the sky like a canopy?

Who has thwarted the plans of the wicked, and set at naught their dark purposes? Who has drawn salvation from the wells of eternity, and breathed new life into men?

Who has put Himself in the place of wretched sinners, and been lifted up their Atonement? Who has triumphed over Death, and seen the light of life, and been satisfied?

Who has taken His seat at the right hand of God, and ever lives to intercede for His own?

Then I turned to see the voice that was speaking to me, and I saw One like the Son of Man

His hair was white, and His eyes like a flame of fire, and His voice like the roar of many waters. *"Fear not,"* He said, and a mighty wave of Life washed over me

At the Revelation of Jesus Christ, Hope of the world, great Lover of my soul

Raise me up to lift my heart and hands in Spirit and in truth to You forever. Amen and Amen.

~TUESDAY~

Lamentations 3:42 "We have transgressed and rebelled, and you have not forgiven."

So much we take for granted, Lord: The sun rising in the sky every morning

The very air we breathe, the stars that grace the evening

The creatures that move along the ground; the plants that fill the earth with green

The opportunity we are given to live each day

We sin against our neighbor and call to You, and You hear in Heaven, and forgive

We are defeated by our enemies for our sin and You hear in Heaven, and forgive

The heavens are shut up with no rain and You hear in Heaven, and forgive

There is pestilence in the land and You hear in Heaven, and forgive

A foreigner in the country prays toward this house and You hear in Heaven, and forgive

We go out to battle and pray toward You and You hear in Heaven, and forgive

We sin against You–for there is no one who does not sin–and You are angry with us and give us into captivity, yet our hearts turn and plead with You, and You hear in Heaven, and forgive

But at what cost did this forgiveness come? For God so loved the world, that You gave Your only Son, that whoever believes in Him should not perish but have everlasting life

When we lift our prayers for forgiveness in this House, this Temple of our flesh in which Your Holy Spirit so marvelously dwells:

Let us remember, Lord, that we were bought with a price, and our bodies are not our own; and glorify You for Your wondrous deeds for men. Amen

~WEDNESDAY~

Lamentations 3:43 "You have wrapped yourself with anger and pursued us, killing without pity"

Life is so fragile, Lord; it passes so quickly

It is fleeting; it cannot be grasped

Like a slave who longs for the shadow, I am allotted months of emptiness

When I lie down, I say, *"When shall I arise?"* But the night is long

My days are swifter than a weaver's shuttle, and come to their end without hope

Remember that my life is a breath; my eyes will never again see good

The eye of him who sees me will behold me no more; while Your eyes are on me, I shall be gone

As a cloud fades and vanishes, so he who goes down to Sheol comes not up

He returns no more to his house, nor does his place know him anymore

What is man, that You make so much of him, that You set Your heart on him, visit him every morning, test him every moment?

But You, O Lord, do not be far off. O You my Help, come quickly to my aid. Deliver my soul from the sword; save me from the mouth of the lion

I will tell of Your Name to my brothers; in the midst of the congregation I will praise You

You who fear the Lord, praise Him! All you offspring of Jacob, glorify Him, and stand in awe of Him, all you offspring of Israel!

For He has not despised the affliction of the afflicted, and has not hidden His face from us

Those who seek Him shall praise the Lord: May your hearts live forever!

They shall proclaim His righteousness to a people yet unborn, for He has done it. Amen.

~THURSDAY~

Lamentations 3:44 "You have wrapped yourself with a cloud so that no prayer can pass through."

We have all known it, Lord

A distance; a silence

A barrenness of soul within

A dry and weary land, where there is no water

A turned shoulder, where once there was acceptance

A veil drawn, where once there was warm welcome

Is it something I have done–or not done? Have I broken Your Law again?

Have I not sought You with all my heart?

The world beckons; the flesh entices; the devil beguiles

But by Your grace I will never again be drawn into their web, for it is nothing but death

Let me remember my song in the night:

Your way, O God, is holy. What god is great like our God? You with Your arm redeemed Your people, the children of Jacob and Joseph. *Selah*

If the ministry of death, carved in letters on stone, came with such glory that the Israelites could not gaze on Moses' face, will not the ministry of the Spirit have even more glory?

Since I have such a hope, I am very bold. When one turns to the Lord, the veil is removed. For where the Spirit of the Lord is, there is freedom

The Spirit of God is upon me, to grant to those who mourn in Zion a beautiful headdress instead of ashes, the oil of gladness instead of mourning, the garment of praise instead of a faint spirit

Lord, it is for You that I wait. Lord, I want to see Jesus. Amen.

~FRIDAY~

Lamentations 3:45 "You have made us scum and garbage among the peoples."

We have lost friends, Lord

We have lost reputation

We have lost cherished dreams

We have lost our seat at the table

We have lost the riches of this world

We have lost our community

We have lost the innocent perspective we once had

We have lost the favor of those in power

And for what? For everything.

You are the Friend of Sinners

You commend us because of the finished work of Christ

You give much to those who have been faithful with little; You set a table for us in the midst of our enemies

You are the great Treasure we spend our lives seeking

You existed in perfect relationship before the dawn of the world; You reveal to us the more excellent way of love

You hung the stars, You saw Satan fall like lightning from Heaven, You command the wind and waves, You raise the dead to new life, You triumphed over Death and the Grave. And Your favor rests on us because of the righteousness of Jesus

We have an Altar from which those who serve the tent have no right to eat

Therefore we will go to You outside the camp, and bear the reproach You endured. Come quickly, Lord Jesus. Amen.

~MONDAY~

Lamentations 3:46 "All our enemies open their mouths against us"

Many bulls encompass me, Lord

Strong bulls of Bashan surround me

They open wide their mouths at me, like a ravening and roaring lion

Dogs encompass me; a company of evildoers encircles me

They divide my garments among them, and for my clothing they cast lots

How did we become mortal enemies? For we once were brothers

The heart of man is a lonely wanderer in the heavens

It pursues what it desires, at whatever cost, to whatever ends

If what the heart really wants is this world, with its riches, its joys, its purposes:

Then it will sacrifice its best and truest friend on that altar, and open its mouth against the truth it once knew, snarling and raging unto its own ruin

But if what the heart really wants is You; Your treasure, Your love, Your will:

Then it will behold the sacrifice You have made of Your only Son, for the propitiation for our sins. And not for ours only but for the sins of the whole world

Worship the Lord in the splendor of holiness

Tremble before Him, all the earth!

Say among the nations, *"The Lord reigns!"*

Bring into His City the glory and honor of the nations, and together lift our hands in joy and praise

To Him who will judge the world in righteousness. For great is the Lord, and greatly to be praised; He is to be feared above all gods. Amen

~TUESDAY~

Lamentations 3:47 "Panic and pitfall have come upon us, devastation and destruction"

All around is loss, Lord. You can see it in people's eyes

Pain that goes deeper than words can tell

Loss that defies description

Disappointment that will not stop gnawing; sorrow that cannot be told

Grief that rises as a shadow dragon over the soul

Sadness that does not go away; distress that runs far beneath the surface

Wounding that has not healed, will not heal

What does one do with all this? What can one ever do?

Truly You have shown me: Take it to the Cross.

For the balm of Your Word that reaches to the depths of who we are

To be filled with the Spirit; to be given a hope that will not disappoint

For comfort in the Gospel of Jesus Christ

For the peace of God that passes all understanding

For a joy that wells up inside us, never to be taken away

For a sure and steadfast anchor of the soul, a hope that enters in behind the curtain

For a light that breaks forth like the dawn, a healing that springs up within

But all these things are incidental, next to the very dying form of One who suffered there for me

My sinful self my only shame, Lord; my glory all the Cross

Amen

~WEDNESDAY~

Lamentations 3:48 "My eyes flow with rivers of tears because of the destruction of the daughter of my people."

It is the people, Lord

The ones who do not know what is going on

The little ones, whose angels always see the face of Your Father in Heaven

I saw all Israel scattered on the hills like sheep without a shepherd

And the Lord said, *"These have no master. Let each return to his home in peace"*

Temptations to sin are sure to come, but woe to the one through whom they come

It would be better for him if a millstone were hung around his neck, and he were cast into the sea, than that he should cause one of these little ones to sin

Pay attention to yourselves!

If your brother sins, rebuke him

And if he repents, forgive him

And if he sins against you seven times in the day

And turns to you seven times, saying, *"I repent"*

You <u>must</u> forgive him

For therein is the destruction of the daughter of my people

It is in our unrepentant sin, and in our unforgiveness

Do we not hold one another in our hands?

Those whom He loves, He rebukes and disciplines. Be earnest therefore, and repent

And forgive one another from the heart, as God in Christ forgave you. Amen

~THURSDAY~

Lamentations 3:49 "My eyes will flow without ceasing, without respite"

They called you the Man of Sorrows, Lord

It was not that You were weak, though they may have thought so

You who removes mountains and overturns them in Your anger

You who shakes the earth out of its place, and its pillars tremble

Who commands the sun and seals up the stars

Who alone stretched out the heavens and trampled the waves of the sea; Who made the Bear and Orion, the Pleiades and the chambers of the south

Who does great things beyond searching out, and marvelous things beyond number

You wept over Jerusalem, for You would have gathered their children together as a hen gathers her brood under her wings; but they would not

You wept at the grave of Your friend, when You saw the fruits of Death

You wept because You loved them

And You went out weeping, bearing the seed for sowing, that You might come home with shouts of joy, bringing Your sheaves with You

What does it mean to follow You, then? It means to let love be genuine; to abhor what is evil, and hold fast to what is good

To love one another with brotherly affection, outdo one another in showing honor, be not slothful in zeal, be fervent in spirit, serve the Lord

To rejoice in hope, be patient in tribulation, be constant in prayer. To bless those who persecute us; to bless and do not curse them

To rejoice with those who rejoice, and weep with those who weep

For there is a Day coming when we shall be comforted. Amen, Lord Jesus, come quickly.

~FRIDAY~

Lamentations 3:50 "Until the Lord from heaven looks down and sees"

B*eer-Lahai-Roi.* You are a God of Seeing, Lord

You saw when Adam and Eve broke Your holy Law and passed from life into death; You saw when Abel fell at the hand of his brother

You saw when Noah walked uprightly in a world full of corruption; You saw when Abraham raised his knife in faith that You would provide a Lamb for the offering

You saw when Hagar fled from the mistreatment of her mistress, the slave fleeing from the free woman

You saw when Jacob wrestled with Your angel, and prevailed; You saw when Joseph's brothers threw him in the pit and sold him into slavery

You saw when Moses left the treasures of Egypt to follow You in the desert; You saw when David fled Jerusalem and his son, and all the land wept aloud with him

You saw when the widow of Zarephath ate her last morsel waiting for Your provision; You saw when the Shunammite woman cried in her grief, *"Did I ask my lord for a son?"*

You saw when Micaiah spoke truth to power and said, *"I saw all Israel scattered on the hills;"* You saw when Isaiah beheld Your glory in the temple, and cried out for his unclean lips

You saw when Jeremiah rebuked the prophets for their appalling false prophecy, and the priests for ruling at their direction; and he said, *"What will you do when the end comes?"*

You saw when all Nineveh repented in dust and ashes, and the only unanswered question was whether the prophet himself would repent; the sign of Jonah in the Resurrection

You saw when the Elijah who was to come called out in the wilderness, *"Prepare the way of the Lord, and make His paths straight;"* And You saw when Your Son cried, *"Father, into Your hands I commit My spirit"*

You are my Refuge, my Portion in the land of the living. Look on me in mercy, Lord. Amen.

~MONDAY~

Lamentations 3:51 "My eyes cause me grief at the fate of all the daughters of my city."

You knew every one, Lord

Created for beauty, created for grace, created for wisdom

Kings' daughters, royal princesses

Theirs was to have been all of Creation to have dominion over, at their husband's side

Mothers of nations

Progenitors of children beyond number

Carrying within them the gentle flame of relational power

Teaching their sons to use their strength to protect life, to serve it, to uplift it

Teaching their daughters to use their beauty to give life, to nurture it, to grow it

Their graceful banner of love lifted over all their own

But when Eve fell, taking for herself the seat of judgment over right and wrong

They fell with her every one, and they have fallen ever since

But for all this, You have not forgotten them in Your redemption

The Lord gives the Word

The women who announce the news are a great host

"The kings of the armies–they flee, they flee!"

The wings of a dove covered with silver, its pinions with shimmering gold

You are our El Shaddai; let Your people be fruitful and multiply, lifting holy hands in worship. Amen

~TUESDAY~

Lamentations 3:52 "I have been hunted like a bird by those who were my enemies without cause"

Who is my enemy, Lord? Is it he who seeks my downfall

Who speaks falsely against Your work in me

Who rejoices when I stumble

Who would entice me into sin

Who does not bless Your Name

Who loves this world, and whose reward will be in it

Who makes provision for the flesh

Who worships the spirit of this age

Who reacts savagely to Your Word, as a brute beast

Who will not seek that holiness without which no one will see the Lord

Who would sacrifice everything and everyone around to his sin

Who makes a golden calf at the foot of the holy Mountain

Who sits down to eat and drink, and rises up to play

Who assembles together at the place that in Hebrew is called Armageddon

Who is my enemy, Lord? God help me, it is I

By Your Spirit's power, help me crucify the flesh, with its passions and desires

To worship God only

To fulfill the Law in one word: To love my neighbor as myself

And to look for Your coming, Jesus. You are my great hope, Lord. Amen

~WEDNESDAY~

Lamentations 3:53 "They flung me alive into the pit and cast stones on me"

I have lost close friends, Lord; I have endured vicious slander

I have seen wickedness prevail over good. I have seen Your holy Word maligned

I have known the reproach of Your Name

I have endured the loss of many things

I have endured the scorn of unbelief

I have received wounds at the house of my friends

I have spoken truth to power and felt its unjust retaliation

But for all this, I have not suffered to the point of shedding blood

Jesus Christ was left alone by all His friends at His death. He endured the force not just of deadly words but of deadly deeds

He went under the waters of judgment without rescue, from the burden of our sin

He Himself was the Word of God, the Logos before time, and men maligned Him

He bore the reproach not just of men but of Your Law, and bore it silently; He endured the loss of all things

He endured the hatred of His brothers, who killed the Heir to the vineyard

It was Your rebuke that broke His heart. Behold, and see if there is any sorrow like His sorrow

He Himself was Truth, and He bore our sins in His body on the Tree, that we might die to sin and live to righteousness

By Your wounds I have been healed, Lord Jesus. Let me see Your glory today. Amen

~THURSDAY~

Lamentations 3:54 "Water closed over my head; I said, 'I am lost.'"

It is too much, Lord. I have sought to know it all

To dig deep into the reasons why

To see behind the veils that were drawn

To understand what had been hidden

What the world took for faithfulness, for wisdom, for virtue

Behind the faithfulness there were subtle lies

Behind the wisdom was foolishness, buried deep in flattery

Behind the virtue was false desire, raging against the iron bars that held it in

And I heard the voice of the Lord saying, *"Whom shall I send, and who will go for us?"*

Then I said, *"Here I am! Send me"*

And He said, *"Go, and say to this people: Keep on hearing, but do not understand*

"Keep on seeing, but do not perceive. Make the heart of this people dull, and their ears heavy, and blind their eyes, lest they see with their eyes, and hear with their ears, and understand with their hearts

And turn and be healed"

Then I said, *"How long, O Lord?"* And He said, *"Until cities lie waste without inhabitant, and houses without people, and the land is a desolate waste, and the Lord removes people far away"*

And when the destroying water of truth closed over my head, I saw a vision of a Holy Seed

The Stump that remained when the tree was felled. Lord Jesus, You are our hope. Amen

~FRIDAY~

Lamentations 3:55 "I called on your name, O Lord, from the depths of the pit"

Lord, You are the One I call to. You are the Resurrection, who died and is alive forevermore

You are the Son of David; blessed is He who comes in the Name of the Lord. You are the Son of Man, who has authority on earth to forgive sins

You are the Bread of Life; whoever comes to You shall not hunger, and whoever believes in You shall never thirst

You are the Light of the World, and whoever follows You will not walk in darkness

You are the Gate for the sheep, who hear Your voice, and You call us by name and lead us out. You are the Good Shepherd, who laid down Your life for the sheep

You are the Resurrection and the Life, and whoever believes in You, though he die, yet shall he live

You are the Way, the Truth, and the Life, and no one comes to the Father except through You. You are the True Vine, and your branches abide in You

You are the Messiah, the suffering Servant, who came to Your own and they did not receive You. You are the Lamb of God, who takes away the sin of the world

You are the Faithful Witness, the Firstborn from the dead, who loves us and has freed us from our sins by Your blood

You are the one Mediator between God and man, the man Christ Jesus, who gave Yourself as a ransom for all

You are the First and the Last, who died and came to life for our salvation. You are the Only Begotten Son, in whom the Father is well pleased; blessed are all who take refuge in You

You are the I Am, whose day Abraham saw and rejoiced, and the Covenant is fulfilled in You

In God I trust; I shall not be afraid. Show me Your glory today, Lord. Amen

~MONDAY~

Lamentations 3:56 "You heard my plea, 'Do not close your ear to my cry for help!'"

If I gain nothing else in my life, Lord; if all men turn their faces from me

If I suffer the loss of all things for Your sake

If my heart is broken for the unfaithfulness of Your people

If the enemy exults over us and the walls are broken down

If Your Word is maligned and my soul is grieved over it

If justice is turned back; if righteousness stands far away; if truth has stumbled in the public squares, and uprightness cannot enter; if truth is lacking

And he who departs from evil makes himself a prey

Then the Lord saw it, and it displeased Him that there was no justice

He saw that there was no man; He wondered that there was no one to intercede

Then His own arm brought Him salvation, and His righteousness upheld Him

He put on righteousness as a breastplate, and a helmet of salvation on His head

According to their deeds, so will He repay, wrath to His adversaries, repayment to His enemies

So shall they fear the Name of the Lord from the west, and His glory from the rising of the sun

For He will come like a rushing stream, which the wind of the Lord drives

"And a Redeemer will come to Zion, to those in Jacob who turn from transgression," declares the Lord. *"My Spirit that is upon you and My words I have put in your mouth, shall not depart from your mouth or the mouth of your offspring, from this time forth and forevermore."* Amen

~TUESDAY~

Lamentations 3:57 "You came near when I called on you; you said, 'Do not fear!'"

You could have turned away from me, Lord. You could have let the Law deal with me

The just deserts of my sin, the righteous penalty for my rebellion against You

The long memory of my journey into the far country

Where I squandered Your property in reckless living

When a severe famine arose, and I began to be in need, when I was hired out at hard labor

Feeding the ever-hungry mouths that gnaw and devour at the soul

Longing to be fed from their trough, but no one gave me anything

Until I came to myself, and remembered that Your servants have more than enough bread, while I perished there with hunger.

And I arose to come to You

To say, *"Father, I have sinned against Heaven and against You. I am no longer worthy to be called Your son*

"Treat me as one of Your hired servants"

But while I was still a long way off, You were filled with compassion. And You ran and embraced me, and kissed me

And called for the best robe to be put on me, and a ring on my hand, and shoes on my feet

And called for the fattened calf to be killed, and that all eat and celebrate

For I Your son was dead, and am alive again; I was lost, and am found

Let me never fear this world again, Father; I am Yours alone. Amen

~WEDNESDAY~

Lamentations 3:58 "You have taken up my cause, O Lord; you have redeemed my life."

I have taken up my own cause, Lord, and what has it done for me?

Sin, sadness

Separation, suffering

Schism

I have repented of trying to be my own Savior, and have turned my face to You

I will give thanks to the Lord, and call upon Your Name

I will make known Your deeds among the peoples

I will sing to You, sing praises to You

I will tell of all Your wondrous works!

I will glory in Your holy Name

Let the hearts of those who seek the Lord rejoice. Seek the Lord and His strength; seek His presence continually

Remember the wondrous works that He has done, His miracles and the judgments He uttered, O offspring of Israel His servant, children of Jacob, His chosen ones

He is the Lord our God; His judgments are in all the earth

Remember His covenant forever, the Word that He commanded, for a thousand generations

The covenant that He made with Abraham; His sworn promise to Isaac, which He confirmed to Jacob as a statute, to Israel as an everlasting covenant

He rebuked kings on their account, saying, *"Touch not Mine anointed ones"*

Sing to the Lord, all the earth! Tell of His salvation from day to day. Amen

~THURSDAY~

Lamentations 3:59 "You have seen the wrong done to me, O Lord; judge my cause."

It was wrong, Lord

The church is supposed to be a hospital–right?

Instead they shoot the wounded

They beat their fellow servants, thinking the Master will not return soon

False under-shepherds feeding only themselves, waterless clouds swept along by the winds

Fruitless trees in late autumn, twice dead, uprooted

They handle Your Word wrongly, with cunning, and with disgraceful, underhanded ways

They refuse to welcome the brothers

They stop those who want to and put them out of the church

They talk wicked nonsense against the brothers

They do not acknowledge spiritual authority

Because they love to be first

O Lord, my heart is not lifted up

My eyes are not raised too high

I do not occupy myself with things too great and too marvelous for me

But I have calmed and quieted my soul, like a weaned child with its mother

Like a weaned child is my soul within me

O Israel, hope in the Lord, from this time forth and forevermore. Amen

~FRIDAY~

Lamentations 3:60 "You have seen all their vengeance, all their plots against me."

You saw it all, Lord

The long season of brotherhood

The many trials we endured together

The joys we knew

The sorrows we shared

The faithfulness we proclaimed

The spiritual attacks we endured

The revelations we received

The power made known among us, the sweet fellowship we enjoyed

And for what? Have I now become their enemy for telling them the truth?

For I do not want You to be unaware of the affliction we experienced. For we were so utterly burdened beyond our strength that we despaired of life itself

Indeed, we felt that we had received the sentence of death. But that was to make us rely not on ourselves but on God who raises the dead

You delivered us from such a deadly peril, and You will deliver us

On You we have set our hope that You will deliver us again

For as we share abundantly in Christ's sufferings, so through Christ we share abundantly in comfort too

Blessed be the God and Father of our Lord Jesus Christ, the Father of all mercies and God of all comfort

Who comforts us in all our affliction

Amen

~MONDAY~

Lamentations 3:61 "You have heard their taunts, O Lord, all their plots against me."

You have heard them all, O Lord, all the taunts:

"If Cain is revenged sevenfold, then Lamech is revenged seventy-sevenfold," Lamech said

The people said, *"Come, let us build a tower, and make a name for ourselves"*

Pharaoh said, *"Who is the Lord, that I should obey him? I will not let Israel go."*

Ahab said to the man of God, *"Is it you, you troubler of Israel?"*

Rabshakeh said to the people on the wall, *"Has any of the gods of the nations ever delivered their people out of my hand?"*

The king's officer said, *"Look, even if the Lord opened the floodgates of the heavens, could such a thing happen?"*

Nebuchadnezzar said, *"Is this not the great Babylon I have built by my own mighty power?*

But mercy triumphs over judgment

Here we have no lasting city, but we seek the City that is to come

The Lord our God brought us out of the land of Egypt, the house of slavery

Your servants proclaimed Your Word, and this world was not worthy of them

Behold, the nations are as a drop in the bucket, as dust on the scales

You performed Your signs and wonders, miracles in the land of Ham

You are Lord of lords and King of kings, and with you are Your called and chosen and faithful

You have prepared us for this very thing, and have given us Your Spirit as a guarantee. Amen

~TUESDAY~

Lamentations 3:62 "The lips and thoughts of my assailants are against me all the day long."

My enemies are arrayed against me, Lord: The world, the flesh, and the devil

They are formidable foes, each one far beyond my own strength

The world has been against You ever since the flaming sword in the Garden

The cares of the world and the deceitfulness of riches choke Your Word

The sons of the world are more shrewd in their dealings than the children of light

The world hates You, and hates us, because by Your Word we testify that its deeds are evil

The flesh has rebelled ever since our mother ate the forbidden fruit. For to set the mind on the flesh is death, but to set the mind on the Spirit is life and peace

The desires of the flesh are against the Spirit, and the desires of the Spirit are against the flesh. And the mind that is set on the flesh is hostile to God's law, and indeed it cannot submit to it

The devil has been crouching at our door since Cain slew his brother Abel. He prowls around like a roaring lion, seeking whom he may devour. He offers us three temptations: The lust of the body, the lust of the eye, the pride of life

Yet here too, Your Word tells us the truth:

"Take heart, for I have overcome the world."

"But put on the Lord Jesus Christ, and make no provision for the flesh, to gratify its desires."

"Be gone, Satan! For it is written, 'You shall worship the Lord your God and Him only shall you serve.'"

Defend me by Your righteous power, O Lord, and I will praise You all the day long. Amen

~WEDNESDAY~

Lamentations 3:63 "Behold their sitting and their rising; I am the object of their taunts."

My God, my God, why have You forsaken me? Why are You so far from saving me, from the words of my groaning?

O my God, I cry by day, but You do not answer; and by night, but I find no rest

Yet You are holy, enthroned on the praises of Israel

In You our fathers trusted; they trusted, and You delivered them

But I am a worm and not a man, scorned by mankind and despised by the people:

"He trusts in the Lord; let Him deliver Him! Let Him rescue Him, for He delights in Him!"

Who has believed our message? And to whom has the arm of the Lord been revealed?

He had no form or majesty that we should look at Him, no beauty that we should desire Him. He was despised and rejected by men, a Man of Sorrows, and acquainted with grief

As One from whom men hide their faces, He was despised, and we esteemed Him not

All we like sheep have gone astray; we have turned every one to his own way, and the Lord has laid on Him the iniquity of us all

O Lord, You have searched me and known me. You know when I sit down and when I rise up; You discern my thoughts from afar

You hem me in, behind and before, and lay Your hand upon Me

Search me, O God, and know my heart! Try me and know my thoughts

See if there be any grievous way in me, and lead me in the Way everlasting. Amen

~THURSDAY~

Lamentations 3:64 "You will repay them, O Lord, according to the work of Your hands."

It is easy to read Your Word, Lord, but it is hard to discern what to do in dark situations

Men's words get tangled up with Yours, and justice is turned back

Righteousness stands far away; truth has stumbled in the public squares, and uprightness cannot enter. Truth is lacking, and he who departs from evil makes himself a prey

What then are the works of the Lord? You formed the world in the dawn of time, and Your Spirit hovered over the waters, Witness to the power of Your Word in all its creative and sovereign glory

You deluged the earth with water, and took the breath of life from every living thing, for sin

You showed Your miracles in the land of Ham, and the gods of Egypt You destroyed. You brought Israel Your firstborn son out of the land of slavery, and brought them into the land of promise

You brought David from tending the sheepfold, and gave him victory over his enemies, and set him on a throne that would not fail. You set up a Temple that would mirror the eternal place of worship

You sent the Anointed One to bring Your people back from their spiritual bondage. A bruised reed He did not break, and a smoldering wick He did not snuff out

He turned the hearts of the parents to their children, and the children to their parents. He destroyed the Temple, prophesying that in three days He would raise it up again

And when the time for judgment had come: You repaid to Him all the punishment for our sin, O Lord, according to the work of Your hands

For from Him and through Him and for Him are all things. To Christ be the glory forever!

Amen

~FRIDAY~

Lamentations 3:65 "You will give them dullness of heart; your curse will be on them."

Lord, of all the admonitions given in this book of Lamentation, this is perhaps the most sobering

We were to have been Your covenant people

You who created us, O Jacob; You who formed us, O Israel. You redeemed us, You called us by name, we were Yours

When we passed through the waters, You would be with us, and through the rivers, they would not overwhelm us

When we walked through fire we would not be burned, because we were precious in Your eyes, and You loved us

But Your people found fault with You, though there was no fault, and we went far from You

The priests did not say, *"Where is the Lord?"* Those who handle the Law did not know You

Has a nation changed its gods–even though they are no gods? But Your people have changed their glory for that which does not profit

Be appalled, O heavens, at this; be shocked, be utterly desolate

Your people have committed two evils: We have forsaken You, the fountain of living waters, and we have hewed out cisterns for ourselves, broken cisterns that can hold no water

For all who rely on works of the Law are under a curse, for it is written: *"Cursed be everyone who does not abide by all things written in the Book of the Law, and do them"*

Christ redeemed us from the curse of the Law by becoming a curse for us, that we might receive the promised Spirit through faith

Remove from us our hearts of stone, and give us hearts of flesh, and be our God

Amen

~MONDAY~

Lamentations 3:66 "You will pursue them in anger and destroy them from under your heavens, O Lord."

We have broken Your holy Law, Lord

The Lord is my light and my salvation; whom shall I fear?

We have forgotten our first love, and gone after other lovers

The Lord is the stronghold of my life; of whom shall I be afraid?

We have neglected Your true worship, and our house is left to us desolate; We have not made return according to Your grace, for our hearts were proud

Though an army shall encamp against me, my heart shall not fear; Though war arise against me, yet I will be confident

The summer is gone, the harvest is past, and we are not saved. We have done foolishly, our hearts have gone far from You

One thing have I asked of the Lord, that will I seek after: That I may dwell in the house of the Lord all the days of my life

We have sinned against Heaven and against You; We are no longer worthy to be called Your Sons

To gaze upon the beauty of the Lord and to inquire in His temple. Cast me not off; forsake me not, O God of my salvation!

For in the hand of the Lord there is a cup, a cup of wrath, and You have drained it to its dregs

Wait for the Lord; be strong, and let your heart take courage. Wait for the Lord

I wept because no one was found who was worthy to open the scroll and look inside it

Weep no more. Behold, the Lion of Judah, the Root of David, has conquered! Worthy is the Lamb who was slain, to receive power and honor and glory and blessing. Amen.

~TUESDAY~

Lamentations 4:1 "How the gold has grown dim, how the pure gold is changed! The holy stones lie scattered at the head of every street."

The voice of one crying in the wilderness: *"Prepare the way of the Lord, and make His paths straight"*

The glory of the Temple has grown dim

The pure gold has been stripped away, and taken as spoils of war

The smoke from the sacrifices no longer rises

The priests no longer intercede for the people

"You brood of vipers!" the prophet cries. *"Produce fruit in keeping with repentance*

And do not presume to say to yourselves, 'We have Abraham as our father'

For I tell you, God is able from these stones to raise up children for Abraham. Even now the axe is laid to the root of the trees

Every tree therefore that does not bear good fruit is cut down and thrown into the fire"

As we come to Him, a living Stone rejected by men but in the sight of God chosen and precious

We ourselves like living stones are being built up as a spiritual house, to be a holy priesthood

To offer spiritual sacrifices acceptable to God through Jesus Christ

For it stands in Scripture: *Behold, I am laying in Zion a stone, a cornerstone chosen and precious, and whoever believes in Him will not be put to shame*

Once we were not a people, but now we are God's people; once we had not received mercy, but now we have received mercy

By faith let Your Spirit build us on the foundation that is Christ, and receive us into glory. Amen

~WEDNESDAY~

Lamentations 4:2 "The precious sons of Zion, worth their weight in fine gold, how they are regarded as earthen pots, the work of a potter's hands!"

Lord, we are made in Your image

Set as stewards over Your Creation

Made a little lower than the angels, crowned with glory and honor

Given dominion over the works of Your hands

All things put under our feet

All sheep and oxen, also the beasts of the field

The birds of the heavens, and the fish of the sea

Whatever passes along the paths of the seas

O Lord, our Lord, how majestic is Your Name in all the earth!

Yet we did not keep Your holy Law, but rebelled against You

We fell from grace

And along with us fell all Creation, and it groans together in the pains of childbirth until now

It is therefore decreed that our salvation shall not be found in our obedience, or in our victory

But in returning and rest we shall be saved; in quietness and trust shall be our strength

Therefore the Lord waits to be gracious to us, and therefore He exalts Himself to show mercy

For the Lord is a God of justice; blessed are all who wait for Him

O Lord, our Lord, how majestic is Your Name in all the earth! We bow before You and worship. Amen

~THURSDAY~

Lamentations 4:3 "Even jackals offer the breast, they nurse their young, but the daughter of my people has become cruel, like the ostriches in the wilderness."

We are yours, Lord; You have ransomed us as Your own

Do we not know that the unrighteous will not inherit the kingdom of God?

Let us not be deceived: Neither the sexually immoral, nor idolaters, nor adulterers, nor men who practice homosexuality

Nor thieves, nor the greedy, nor drunkards, nor revilers, nor swindlers will inherit the kingdom of God

And such were some of us

But we were washed

We were sanctified

We were justified in the Name of the Lord Jesus Christ

And by the Spirit of our God

For by grace we have been saved through faith, and this is not our own doing; it is the gift of God

Not of works, so that no one may boast

For we are Your workmanship, created in Christ Jesus for good works

Which God prepared beforehand, that we should walk in them

To us God has chosen to make known how great among the Gentiles are the riches of the glory of this mystery

Which is Christ in us, the hope of glory

Lord Jesus, let the beauty of Your holiness be seen in me today, that all might worship You. Amen

~FRIDAY~

Lamentations 4:4 "The tongue of the nursing infant sticks to the roof of its mouth for thirst; the children beg for food, but no one gives to them."

Lord, You said that we should not live by bread alone, but by every word that proceeds from the mouth of God

Your Word is life

It is light

It is God-breathed, and profitable for teaching

It is truth

The grass withers, the flower fades, but the Word of our God will stand forever

Yet Your sheep are not fed with it

"Do not preach"–thus they preach–*"one should not preach of such things. Disgrace will not overtake us"*

Should this be said, O house of Jacob? Has the Lord grown impatient? Are these His deeds?

Do not My words do good to him who walks uprightly? But lately My people have risen up as an enemy

Arise and go, for this is no place to rest, because of uncleanness that destroys!

If a man should go about and utter wind and lies, saying, *"I will preach to you of wine and strong drink,"* he would be the preacher for this people

I will surely assemble all of you, O Jacob; I will gather the remnant of Israel. I will set them together like sheep in a fold, like a flock in its pasture

He who opens a breach goes up before them; their King passes on before them, their Lord at their head

Lord God of all, feed us with the true food of Your very self, that we may abide in You. Amen

~MONDAY~

Lamentations 4:5 "Those who once feasted on delicacies perish in the streets; those who were brought up in purple embrace ash heaps."

We were children of the King, Lord. Your blessing was on us

The warm sun shone on our heads; the work of our hands prospered

Our enemies always fell before our advance, and the stone walls stood firm around our city

Your priests remembered Your Name, and led us in worship up the steps of Your holy temple

Treasures were brought out of Your storehouse, and we reveled in Your grace

Crops grew tall and barns were filled to overflowing

Until the evil day when lies were exchanged for the truth

Your worship was corrupted, and fire devoured the unholy

Your prophets grew silent and the priests barred the doors to the Holy Place

The walls were torn down, the fields scorched and bare

Why was the sign of royalty taken from us, our lamp blown out? How did we go so far astray?

Because we forgot You, Lord. We presumed on Your goodness and grace and we did not listen to Your Word

We quenched Your Spirit and mocked the eternal truth of Your Law. We took Your good gifts without a second thought for You, the Giver

And it took the pain of loss to realize what we had done

As for me, I said: *"O Lord, be gracious to me; heal me, for I have sinned against You"*

Blessed be the Lord, the God of Israel, from everlasting to everlasting. Amen and Amen

~TUESDAY~

Lamentations 4:6 "For the chastisement of the daughter of my people has been greater than the punishment of Sodom, which was overthrown in a minute, and no hands were wrung for her."

We truly do think we are different, Lord. We have received from His fullness, grace upon grace

For the Law was given through Moses, but grace and truth came through Jesus Christ

And no one has ever seen God. The only God, who is at the Father's side, He has made Him known

And the Word became flesh and dwelt among us, and we have seen His glory

Glory as of the only Son from the Father, full of grace and truth

Yet for all this, how sick is our heart! Behold, everyone who uses proverbs will use this proverb about us: *Like mother, like daughter*

Our mother was a Hittite and our father was an Amorite. Our elder sister was Samaria, and our younger sister was Sodom

And for our sins we have become an object of reproach, for with our unfaithfulness we have made our sinful sisters appear righteous

Will we be exalted to Heaven? No, we will be brought down to Hades, without Your mercy

For if the mighty works that have been done in us had been done in Sodom, she would have remained unto this day

We have presumed on the riches of His kindness and forbearance and patience, not knowing that God's kindness is meant to lead us to repentance

When the bodies of our witnesses lie slain on the streets of that great city where our Lord was crucified, that symbolically is called Sodom and Egypt, may they not rejoice over us

May the breath of life from God enter into us, and may we stand up again in the power of the Resurrection

Amen, Lord. Come quickly

~WEDNESDAY~

Lamentations 4:7 "Her princes were purer than snow, whiter than milk; their bodies were more ruddy than coral, the beauty of their form was like sapphire."

The loss is bitter beyond words, Lord

They were Your sons, princes over Your people. They spoke Your Word with authority

They ministered Your grace; they led us to sing Your praises, with hands held high to glorify You

Enemies fell before us, strongholds were demolished; Your Kingdom went forward and lives were changed

The wayward were admonished, the weary were attended, the sick at heart encouraged. Your Church grew beautiful, powerful, terrible as an army with banners

But her princes grew proud, and their eyes darkened before You. Their word became higher than Your Word

Their favor more sought after than Your grace

Their praises were spoken more readily than Yours, with hands held out to receive payment

The enemy slowly built a stronghold among Your people. Another kingdom was furthered, built on the pursuit of money, power, and image

The wayward were rewarded, the weary were thrown aside, the sick at heart crushed

Your Church gave her beauty to another, and forgot her Bridegroom

So Your firstborn Son, the true Prince came to ransom His people, His sister, His bride, to draw unto Himself all whom the Father has given Him

Daughters of Jerusalem, I charge you, do not awaken love until it so desires

The Lover of my soul is mine and I am His; blessed be His Name

Amen

~THURSDAY~

Lamentations 4:8 "Now their face is blacker than soot; they are not recognized in the streets; their skin has shriveled on their bones; it has become as dry wood."

Lord, the fool says in his heart, *"There is no God"*

They are corrupt, doing abominable iniquity; there is none who does good

God looks down from Heaven on the children of man, to see if there are any who understand, who seek after God

They have all fallen away; together they have become corrupt

There is none who does good

Not even one

It is You, and You alone, that will be our salvation

For You are good

You are holy

You are just; You are merciful

You are compassionate

You freely forgive

You pour out on us richly through Jesus Christ our Savior

You justify us by Your grace

You make us heirs according to the hope of eternal life

The saying is trustworthy, and we insist on these things

So that those who have believed in God may devote themselves to good works

Lord Jesus, our eyes are on You. Amen

~FRIDAY~

Lamentations 4:9 "Happier were the victims of the sword than the victims of hunger, who wasted away, pierced by lack of the fruits of the field."

All our lives we have pursued our hunger, Lord, our daily need to be filled

Our desire for youth, for strength, for beauty; our sharp craving for the things of this world

The void of emptiness yawning through all of our words and actions

Our longing for fulfillment, to swallow up the thorns with thick wheat, to bear life without pain. And in a great irony this hunger consumes us, it devours us

So foolish are we that we will not go to the wellspring of life to drink

We will not receive purpose from the hands of our Creator; we will not take Your yoke upon us, though it is easy, and Your burden is light

Our fathers ate the manna in the wilderness; but our true Father gives us Bread from Heaven. You said to us, *"I am the Bread of Life*

"Whoever comes to Me shall not hunger, and whoever believes in Me shall never thirst"

Your food was to do the will of Him who sent you and to accomplish His work

You stepped willingly into our place, to suffer and to die for sins once for all

You became the victim of the sword for us. And when in the power of an indestructible life You rose again, You led captives in Your train

For the gift You have given – to us – to me – is eternal life

This is eternal life, that they know You, the only true God, and Jesus Christ whom You have sent

Holy Spirit, rise up within me today to speak with joy of such a great salvation

And bring many sons and daughters to glory. Amen

~MONDAY~

Lamentations 4:10 "The hands of compassionate women have boiled their own children; they became their food during the destruction of the daughter of my people."

Some griefs are too strong to be spoken, Lord

Some sins too dark even to be named among us

Sin divides. It crushes and destroys

Like a cancer it spreads, growing without hesitation or consideration

It eats us from the inside out

It mars the Image we were made in, turning us into our own self-serving idols at which we would have all others bow down

Offering fulfillment and desire, sin is the bringer of death, death to us and to all around

But for all that, our death is not the greatest wrong that comes of sin

Sin is an offense against Your glory

It is a rebellion against Your holy Law

It is a failure to live a life of worship, drawn by Your beauty, captivated by Your love

It is the fateful rejection of the true Source of all life

Search me, O God, and know my heart

Try me and know my thoughts!

See if there be any grievous way in me, and lead me in the Way everlasting

Bought with the precious blood of Christ, like that of a Lamb without blemish or spot

And of Your great mercy, make me holy, as You are holy. Amen

~TUESDAY~

Lamentations 4:11 "The Lord gave full vent to his wrath; he poured out his hot anger, and he kindled a fire in Zion that consumed its foundations."

I do not understand Your anger, Lord. It is too great for me, too awful to comprehend

My own anger is short-lived

It is often misdirected. It is not purely centered on holiness and truth

My anger does not bring about the righteousness of God

For I cannot see into the heart. I cannot tell the difference between woundedness and malice

But like a white-hot flame, Your wrath searches the farthest corners of being

It separates the wheat from the tares, in that great Day when the hearts of men are winnowed. It reveals what is a waterless spring, a mist driven by the storm, blemishes reveling in deception

When the heavens pass away with a roar, and the heavenly bodies burned up and dissolved

Oh, that You would hide me in Sheol, and conceal me until Your wrath has passed!

Buried with Him in baptism, in which we were also raised with Him through faith in God

And we, who were dead in our trespasses and sins, God has made alive together with Him, canceling the record of debt with its legal demands. This He set aside, nailing it to the Cross of Christ

On Whom the wrath of God was poured out, the cup drained to its very dregs. Your wrath has swept over Him, and Your waves have overwhelmed Him. *Selah*

So that the proven genuineness of our faith in Him might come forth as gold

And result in praise and glory and honor at the revelation of Jesus Christ. Amen

~WEDNESDAY~

Lamentations 4:12 "The kings of the earth did not believe, nor any of the inhabitants of the world, that foe or enemy could enter the gates of Jerusalem."

You have been faithful, Lord, since time began

You have kept Your promises

You have worked Your sovereign will

Your Spirit has been with Your people

You have given Your Word power, and upheld it before all

You have punished evil; You have rewarded those who earnestly seek You

You have revealed Your holy Name

You have defended those who call on You

Yet for all this, we have presumed on Your grace

We have not been faithful to Your worship

We have not depended on Your promises

We have not yielded to Your will in all things

We have not listened to Your Spirit; we have not obeyed Your Word

We have done evil

We have sought You halfheartedly, or not at all

We have taken Your Name in vain; we have not called on You for deliverance

And the gates of the holy City have been overrun

Our soul clings to You; Your right hand upholds us. Of Your great mercy, deliver us, Lord

Amen

~THURSDAY~

Lamentations 4:13 "This was for the sins of her prophets and the iniquities of her priests, who shed in the midst of her the blood of the righteous."

Son of man, prophesy against the shepherds of Israel. Prophesy and say to them, even to the shepherds:

Thus says the Lord God: Ah, shepherds of Israel who have been feeding yourselves!

Should not shepherds feed the sheep?

You eat the fat, you clothe yourselves with the wool, you slaughter the fat ones, but you do not feed the sheep

The weak you have not strengthened, the sick you have not healed, the injured you have not bound up

The strayed you have not brought back, the lost you have not sought, and with force and harshness you have ruled them

My sheep were scattered; they wandered over all the mountains and on every high hill

The priests did not say, *"Where is the Lord?"* Those who handle the Law did not know Me; the shepherds transgressed against Me

The prophets prophesied by Baal and went after things that do not profit

A voice–the cry of the shepherds, and the wail of the lords of the flock! For the Lord is laying waste their pasture, and the peaceful folds are devastated

And He took from the Lord's hand the cup of the wine of wrath, and He drank it. He took the punishment that should have been ours

Like a Lamb that is led to the slaughter, He opened not His mouth

Jesus left the ninety and nine, and sought me until He found me. And He brought me home

"Do you love Me more than these?" Yes, Lord, You know that I love You. *"Feed My lambs."* Amen, Lord

~FRIDAY~

Lamentations 4:14 "They wandered, blind, through the streets; they were so defiled with blood that no one was able to touch their garments."

To be clean, Lord; to know the approval of the holy Law

For all men to know that we are Your children

To have no bloodguiltiness, that there be no condemnation. To at last be free from the many defilements of sin

Free from the heavy burdens, hard to bear, tied up and left on the shoulders of the innocent

Free from shutting the door to the kingdom of Heaven in men's faces

Free from false oaths that delude and blind

Free from straining out the gnat and swallowing the camel

Free from cleaning the outside of the cup, while inside it is full of greed and self-indulgence

Free from the whitewashed tombs full of hypocrisy and lawlessness

Free from all the righteous blood shed on earth, from righteous Abel to Zechariah, murdered between the sanctuary and the altar

O Jerusalem, Jerusalem, the city that kills the prophets and stones those who are sent to it

How often would I have gathered your children together, as a hen gathers her brood under her wings

Yet you were not willing. See, your house is left to you desolate

For I tell you, you will not see Me again, until you say, *"Blessed is He who comes in the Name of the Lord"*

Until you meet Me wandering through the streets, defiled with blood, the sacrificial Lamb bearing the sin of the world, and in true faith touch the hem of My robe. Amen

~MONDAY~

Lamentations 4:15 "Away! Unclean!" people cried at them. "Away! Away! Do not touch!" So they became fugitives and wanderers; people said among the nations, "They shall stay with us no longer."

To speak truth is to be alone, Lord; it is to be hated by all

You have taught us this

For there is no truth in their mouth; their inmost self is destruction

Their throat is an open grave

They flatter with their tongue

But You are not a God who delights in wickedness. Evil may not dwell with You

The boastful shall not stand before Your eyes

You hate all evildoers

You destroy those who speak lies; the Lord abhors the bloodthirsty and deceitful man

"Depart ye; it is unclean" is the cry that goes up before us

Make them bear their guilt, O God

Let them fall by their own counsels

But let all who take refuge in You rejoice

Let them ever sing for joy

And spread Your protection over them

That those who love Your Name may exult in You

For You bless the righteous, O Lord

You cover Him with favor as with a shield. Amen

~TUESDAY~

Lamentations 4:16 "The Lord himself has scattered them; he will regard them no more; no honor was shown to the priests, no favor to the elders."

We come into this world alone, Lord, and we will leave it that way

So much of our lives we spend heaping up wealth, not knowing who will gather

Possessions to show our worth; the favor of those the world deems more important

The appearance of success, the veneer of satisfaction

Money, that universal key that unlocks doors to warm welcome

Friends who compliment us for our good sense in choosing their company

Yet in the midst of all these riches there is a great warning given, quiet but deadly

A voice that says, *"Take care, and be on your guard against all covetousness. For a man's life does not consist in the abundance of his possessions"*

We have said to our soul, *"Soul, you have ample goods laid up for many years; take your ease, eat, drink, be merry"*

Fool! This very night your soul is required of you, and the things you have prepared, whose will they be?

Instead, seek first the Kingdom of God and His righteousness, and these things will be added to you

Fear not, little flock, for it is your Father's good pleasure to give you the Kingdom

Sell your possessions, and give to the needy. Provide yourselves with a treasure in the heavens that does not fail

And when the Day of Judgment comes, you will have a place of refuge

For He comes to cast fire on the earth, and would that it were already kindled! Come quickly, Lord Jesus. Amen

~WEDNESDAY~

Lamentations 4:17 "Our eyes failed, ever watching for help; in our watching we watched for a nation that could not save."

Lord, our hope has grown dim; our eyes have failed watching for help

O God, why do You cast off forever? Why does Your anger smoke against the sheep of Your pasture?

The nations we trusted in have not delivered us

Remember Mount Zion, where you have dwelt

They have forgotten us, and we are left desolate

Direct Your steps to the perpetual ruins; the enemy has destroyed everything in the sanctuary

The light no longer dawns; the darkness is all around us. We have not the wisdom or the strength to deliver ourselves; we are left alone

They set Your sanctuary on fire; they profaned the dwelling place of Your Name. There is no longer any prophet, and there is none among us who knows how long

In sorrow and longing we return to You, the only Lover of our souls. Forgive us, rebuke us, restore us, cleanse us, shape us, make us into Your image again

Yet God my King is from of old, working salvation in the midst of the earth. Do not deliver the soul of Your dove to the wild beasts

If all else passes away, we would see Your face, Lord; a vision of life and truth forever

Have regard for the covenant, for the dark places of the land are full of the habitations of violence

For You we will wait in silence, and in the morning we will sing of Your grace

Let the poor and needy praise Your Name. Arise, O God, defend Your cause!

Amen

~THURSDAY~

Lamentations 4:18 "They dogged our steps so that we could not walk in our streets; our end drew near; our days were numbered, for our end had come."

Our days pass by as a dream, Lord

We are caught up with so many things:

The tyranny of the urgent

Anxiety over what could be

Concern for the unknown

Making sure others think well of us

Possessions that possess us

Maintaining our appearance, even as it fades away

What we will eat, what we will drink

Our body, what we will put on. Is not life more than food, and the body more than clothing?

Look at the birds of the air: They neither sow nor reap nor gather into barns, and yet our heavenly Father feeds them

Consider the lilies of the field, how they grow: They neither toil nor spin, yet Solomon in all his splendor was not arrayed like one of these. Are we not of more value than they?

But let us seek first the Kingdom of God and His righteousness, and all these things will be added to us

For there is only one thing needful: That we may dwell in the house of the Lord all the days of our life

To gaze upon the beauty of the Lord, and to inquire in His temple

The End of all things is at hand; let us willingly go where His Spirit leads. Amen

~FRIDAY~

Lamentations 4:19 "Our pursuers were swifter than the eagles in the heavens; they chased us on the mountains; they lay in wait for us in the wilderness."

Lord, for Your sake we have endured all things

Condemnation from the world, danger from false brothers

The weakness and rebellion of our flesh, the old nature set against Your ways

The loss of dreams, of fond hopes we have seen fade away. The loss of friends, of ones our very souls had been knit to, who have turned away from us

The loss of goods, of possessions in this world we have let go

The constant humbling that comes from walking close with You, as we crucify the flesh again and again. The pursuit is relentless, and we are not enough for it

So if we must boast, then, we will boast of the things that show our weakness. We consider our Lord who endured from sinners such hostility against Himself

He who was in the world, which was made by Him, yet the world did not know Him. He who was betrayed by his own disciple to death and crucifixion

He who wept in the Garden, yet followed the will of His Father to the very end

He who after the suffering of His soul, saw the light of life and was satisfied. He who was alone when all men had turned from Him, yet in the Father was not alone

He who had no place to lay His head, yet by His poverty made us rich

He who endured the Cross, scorning its shame, and is seated at the right hand of God's throne

Our great High Priest who has gone through the heavens and now lives to intercede for us

Through the wilderness You have called us, Lord Jesus, and by Your Spirit we will follow You even to the end of the age. Amen

~MONDAY~

Lamentations 4:20 "The breath of our nostrils, the Lord's anointed, was captured in their pits, of whom we said, 'Under his shadow we shall live among the nations.'"

We have put our hope in many, Lord: The young, the strong, the beautiful

Those who could stand against the storm of time and not be ravaged by it; who could contend with our enemies in the gate and overcome them

Who spoke words that lifted up our souls and captured our hearts, shining like the face of God

We followed them, we revered them, we loved them. They gave us our identity, and we gave them the praise they longed for

They fed the subtle flames of our fears, and we did not question their strange fire in worship. They gave us the community we most longed for, and we turned a blind eye when sheep went missing from the fold

God spoke to us in our prosperity, but we said, "I will not listen." The wind has shepherded all our shepherds, and our lovers have gone into captivity

I came to My garden, My sister, My bride

I sought Him, but found Him not; I called Him, but He gave no answer

Who is this coming up from the wilderness, leaning on her Beloved?

I am my Beloved's, and His desire is for me

Who is this who looks down like the dawn, beautiful as the moon, bright as the sun, terrible as an army with banners?

Set me as a seal upon Your heart, for love is strong as death

Where has your Beloved gone, O most beautiful among women?

Behold, He is coming with the clouds, and every eye will see Him

Remember me, Lord Jesus, when You come into Your kingdom. Amen

~TUESDAY~

Lamentations 4:21 "Rejoice and be glad, O daughter of Edom, you who dwell in the land of Uz; but to you also the cup shall pass; you shall become drunk and strip yourself bare."

You created us with dignity, Lord; we have born Your image since we took our first breath

Created to be Your stewards, to be fruitful and multiply, subduing the earth and having dominion over it, over the fish of the sea, the birds of the air, and every living thing that moves on the earth

You saw everything You had made, and behold, it was good. But when we transgressed Your holy Law, all of Creation was plunged into darkness and death

And we have lived in separation and rebellion against You ever since

And the Lord spoke thus to me with His strong hand upon me, and warned me not to walk in the way of this people, saying:

"Do not call conspiracy all that this people calls conspiracy, and do not fear what they fear. But the Lord of hosts, Him you shall honor as holy. Let Him be your fear, and Him be your dread

And He will become a sanctuary, a stone of offense, a rock of stumbling to both houses of Israel. And many shall stumble on it; they shall fall and be broken; they shall be snared and taken

For in the hand of the Lord there is a cup with foaming wine, well mixed. And He pours out from it, and all the wicked of the earth shall drain it down to its dregs"

For not from the east or the west, and not from the wilderness comes lifting up. But it is God who executes judgment, putting down one and lifting up another

Worthy are You to take the scroll and to open its seals, for You were slain, and by Your blood You ransomed a people for God from every tribe and language and people and nation

And You have made them a kingdom and priests to our God, and they shall reign on the earth. To Him who sits on the throne and to the Lamb be blessing and honor and glory and might forever and ever! Amen

~WEDNESDAY~

Lamentations 4:22 "The punishment of your iniquity, O daughter of Zion, is accomplished; he will keep you in exile no longer; but your iniquity, O daughter of Edom, he will punish; he will uncover your sins."

There are worse things than exile, Lord; much worse

It was grievous, and we still bear the scars from it. We would not listen to You, and would not do all Your commandments

We spurned your statutes; We abhorred Your rules in our soul

We would not do all Your commandments, but broke Your covenant. And You did all that You had told Moses Your servant You would:

You visited us with panic; You made us sow our seed in vain, for our enemies ate it. You set Your face against us, and we were struck down before our enemies

You made those who hated us rule over us, and we fled when none pursued

You broke the pride of our power, and disciplined us sevenfold for our sins

You made our heavens like iron and our earth like bronze

You walked contrary to us in fury, and cast our dead bodies upon the dead bodies of our idols; yet we live. How is it that we live, after all this?

Because we took refuge under the wings of Your Son, and all Your righteous wrath was spent on Him, at the Cross, where our hearts were broken to sin forever

What is the difference between us and the daughters of Edom? There is none

It is all of grace.

"Jacob have I loved," You said, *"and Esau have I hated"*

You love when one repents, and turns from sin, and walks in faith; You hate when one destroys his own immortal soul for a bowl of beans

Blessed be your Name, Lord. Amen

~THURSDAY~

Lamentations 5:1 "Remember, O Lord, what has befallen us; look, and see our disgrace!"

The oracle concerning Babylon, which Isaiah son of Amoz saw:

"On a bare hill raise a signal; cry aloud to them. Wave the hand for them to enter the gates of the nobles

I myself have summoned My mighty men to execute My anger

The sound of a tumult is on the mountains, as of a great multitude; the sound of an uproar of kingdoms, of nations gathering together

The Lord of hosts is mustering a host for battle. They come from a distant land, from the end of the heavens

The Lord and the weapons of His indignation, to destroy the whole land"

Wail, for the Day of the Lord is near! As destruction from the Almighty it will come

Therefore all hands will be feeble, and every human heart will melt. They will be dismayed; pangs and agony will seize them

Behold, the Day of the Lord comes, cruel, with wrath and fierce anger, to make the land a desolation and to destroy its sinners from it. The sun will be dark at its rising, and the moon will not shed its light

And Babylon, glory of kingdoms, will be like Sodom and Gomorrah when God overthrew them

"How art thou fallen from Heaven, O Lucifer, son of the morning! How art thou cut down to the ground, which laid the nations low!

You said in your heart, 'I will ascend to Heaven, above the stars of God; I will make myself like the Most High'

But you are brought down to Sheol, to the far reaches of the pit"

But the Lord has founded Zion, and in her the afflicted of His people find refuge. Amen

~FRIDAY~

Lamentations 5:2 "Our inheritance has been turned over to strangers, our homes to foreigners."

Your judgment has come, O Lord. Behold, the Lord will empty the earth and make it desolate, and He will twist its surface and scatters its inhabitants

And it shall be, as with the people, so with the priest; as with the slave, so with his master

The earth mourns and withers; the highest people of the earth languish. The earth lies defiled under its inhabitants, for they have violated the everlasting covenant

Therefore a curse devours the earth. The wine mourns, the vine languishes, and all the merry-hearted sigh

The mirth of the tambourines is stilled, the noise of the jubilant has ceased. All joy has grown dark; the gladness of the earth is banished. For cursed is everyone who is hanged on a tree

All joy grew dark, for Your face was turned from Him. The music of the angels at His birth was silenced, as all Creation shuddered at His death

He drank of the cup of the fury of Your righteous wrath, and drained it to its dregs. And this curse devoured Him as He suffered: *King of the Jews*

The earth lay defiled under His blood, for they knew not what they did to Him

The ground was split apart at His death, and the curtain to the Holy of Holies rent in two. The Master of the Universe stepped into the punishment of the disobedient slave

The One anointed in the order of Melchizedek went silent as a lamb to the slaughter. And they feared greatly, saying, *"Truly this was the Son of God!"*

But now in Christ Jesus we who once were far off have been brought near by the blood of Christ

In You we are being built together into a dwelling place for God, by the Spirit. Amen and Amen

~MONDAY~

Lamentations 5:3 "We have become orphans, fatherless; our mothers are like widows."

A wandering Aramean was my father

Few and evil have been my days, Lord. Gone are the vain imaginations of youth, the boasts of early strength

Nothing is left of the fat years, the days that passed by as lightly as the summer's breeze

The comforting nights that promised rest, and a dawn after the darkness

What has become of all the cherished hopes and dreams? They have vanished away like smoke on the water

How long, O Lord? Will You hide Yourself forever?

How long will Your wrath burn like fire? Remember how short my time is

For what vanity You have created all the children of man! What man can live, and never see death?

Who can deliver his soul from the power of Sheol? *Selah*

Lord, where is Your steadfast love of old, which by Your faithfulness You swore to David?

Who is this who comes from Edom, in crimsoned garments from Bozrah? *"It is I, speaking in righteousness, mighty to save"*

Why is Your apparel red, and Your garments like His who treads in the winepress? *"I have trodden the winepress alone, and from the peoples no one was with Me"*

I will recount the steadfast love of the Lord, the praises of the Lord. For He said, *"Surely they are My people, children who will not deal falsely"*

In His love and pity He redeemed them; He lifted them up and carried them all the days of old. And He became their Savior

Amen

~TUESDAY~

Lamentations 5:4 "We must pay for the water we drink; the wood we get must be bought."

Lord, we are a generation of merchants

"Today or tomorrow," we say, *"we will go into such and such a town, and spend a year there, and trade, and make profit"*

Yet we do not know what tomorrow will bring. What is our life? For we are a mist that appears for a little time and then vanishes

Instead we ought to say, *"If the Lord wills, we will live and do this or that"*

As it is, we boast in our arrogance, and we accumulate possessions

We suppose we are finding our place in the world, when the world is finding its place in us

We do all from selfish ambition or conceit; we look to our own interests, not those of others

We suppose that it is to no purpose that the Scripture tells of Your Spirit yearning jealously

Our riches have rotted and our garments are moth-eaten; our gold and silver have corroded, and as evidence against us they eat our flesh like fire

We have laid up treasure in the last days. Behold, the wages of the laborers who mowed our fields, kept back by fraud, are crying out against us

And above all this the call of Your blessed Gospel of grace still sounds:

"Come, everyone who thirsts, come to the waters, and he who has no money, come, buy and eat

Incline your ear, and come to Me; hear Me that your soul may live"

What do I have that I have not received? It is all of grace

Lord Jesus, teach me to treasure the free gift of eternal life above all things. Amen

~WEDNESDAY~

Lamentations 5:5 "Our pursuers are at our necks; we are weary; we are given no rest."

Lord, You said to us: *"In returning and rest you shall be saved; in quietness and trust shall be your strength"*

But we were unwilling, and we said, *"No! We will flee upon horses"*

Therefore You decreed that we should flee away

And we said, *"We will ride upon swift steeds"*

Therefore our pursuers have been swift

A thousand have fled at the threat of one, until we were left like a flagstaff at the top of a mountain, like a signal on a hill

"Ah, stubborn children," You declared, *"who carry out a plan, but not Mine; who make an alliance, but not of My Spirit"*

For we were a rebellious people, lying children; children unwilling to hear the instruction of the Lord, who said to the seers: *"Do not see"*

And to the prophets: *"Do not prophesy to us what is right; speak to us smooth things, prophesy illusions, leave the Way, turn aside from the path, let us hear no more about the Holy One of Israel"*

Listen to me, you who pursue righteousness, you who seek the Lord! Look to the rock from which you were hewn

Look to Abraham your father, and to Sarah who bore you, for he was but one when I called him

For they drank from the spiritual Rock that followed them, and the Rock was Christ

Behold, a King will reign in righteousness. He will be like a hiding place from the wind, like streams of water in a dry place, like the shadow of a great Rock in a weary land

Blessed are all who take refuge in Him. Amen

~THURSDAY~

Lamentations 5:6 "We have given the hand to Egypt, and to Assyria, to get bread enough."

Lord, who is the man so wise that he can understand this? To whom has the mouth of the Lord spoken, that he may declare it?

Why is the land ruined and laid waste like a wilderness, so that no one passes through?

And the Lord says: *"Because they have forsaken My Law that I set before them, and have not obeyed my voice or walked in accordance with it*

But have stubbornly followed their own hearts and have gone after the Baals, as their fathers taught them"

Therefore thus says the Lord of hosts, the God of Israel: *"Behold, I will feed this people with bitter food, and give them poisonous water to drink. I will scatter them among the nations whom neither they nor their fathers have known*

"And I will send the sword after them, until I have consumed them"

It was into all this ruin that You came, Lord, when You took our humanity upon You

You kept the Law perfectly and obeyed the voice of the Father. You did not follow Your own heart, but said, *"Thy will be done"*

And although Your food was to do the will of Him who sent You and accomplish His work

You ate the bitter food of exile on our behalf, and You drank the cup of judgment for us. You were stricken and scattered for us as a lamb led to the slaughter

Who can speak of Your descendants? For You were cut off from the land of the living. The sword consumed You, and Your head went under the waves

And You said, *"Whoever feeds on My flesh and drinks My blood has eternal life, and I will raise him up at the last Day"*

Lord, give us this bread always. We lift our eyes to You today. Amen

FRIDAY

Lamentations 5:7 "Our fathers sinned, and are no more; and we bear their iniquities."

Lord, You have written us no new commandment, but an old commandment we had from the beginning:

That whoever says he abides in Him, ought to walk in the same way in which He walked

But who among us is enough for this? Our fathers, godly as they may have been, passed down the same iniquities visited on them:

Hating our brothers, walking in darkness

Walking in untruth, deceiving ourselves

Saying we have not sinned, making Him a liar

Bearing the image of the man of dust

Have mercy, Lord, and sow among us the resurrection of the dead

Sow it among us as perishable, that we may be raised imperishable

Sow it in dishonor, that we may be raised in glory

Sow it in weakness, that we may be raised in power

Sow it among our natural bodies, that we may be raised spiritual beings

For the last Adam has become a life-giving spirit, that we may at last bear the image of the Man of Heaven

Loving as He loved, walking in light, speaking the truth, glorifying God the Father, who is well pleased in His only Son

And we all, with unveiled face, beholding the glory of the Lord, are being transformed into the same image from glory to glory

Even as by the Spirit of the Lord. The Spirit and the Bride say, *"Come."*

Amen

~MONDAY~

Lamentations 5:8 "Slaves rule over us; there is none to deliver us from their hand."

We have been given over, Lord; given over to our unlawful desires

Given over to exile

Given over to unjust rulers

Far from the land we grew to love

The land of promise, the home sworn to Abraham, Isaac, and Jacob

Because of our unfaithfulness to You and our stubborn unbelief

And You command us in our punishment–

Thus says the Lord of hosts, the God of Israel, to all the exiles sent from Jerusalem to Babylon:

"Build houses and live in them, plant gardens and eat their produce

Take wives and have sons and daughters

Take wives for your sons, and give your daughters in marriage, that they may bear sons and daughters

Multiply there, and do not decrease

But seek the welfare of the city where I have sent you into exile, and pray to the Lord on its behalf

For in its welfare you will find your welfare."

By the rivers of Babylon we sat and wept, when we remembered Zion

How shall we sing the Lord's song in a foreign land? If I forget you, O Jerusalem, may my right hand forget its skill

Remember, O Lord, the Day of Jerusalem. We will wait for You, surely wait for You. Amen

~TUESDAY~

Lamentations 5:9 "We get our bread at the peril of our lives, because of the sword in the wilderness."

What do you do with a wilderness, Lord?

A place of which we say, *"It is a waste without man or beast"*

Where the cities of Judah and the streets of Jerusalem are desolate, without flocks or herds

Where the voices of bride and bridegroom are not heard

Where crops do not grow

Where people do not build houses, or tend vineyards, or plant trees

Where the land is not rich, and water does not flow

Where the wind shall shepherd all of our shepherds, and the lovers go into captivity. What do You do with it?

Thus says the Lord who made the earth, the Lord who formed it to establish it–the Lord is His Name:

"Call to Me, and I will answer you, and show you great and mighty things you have not known. I will restore the fortunes of Judah and of Israel, and rebuild them as they were at first

"And this city shall be to Me a name of joy, a praise and a glory before all nations"

Give thanks to the Lord of hosts, for the Lord is good, for His steadfast love endures forever!

"And the flocks shall again pass under the hands of the one who counts them," says the Lord. We are the sheep of Your pasture; we hear Your voice, and we know You, and we follow You

You give us eternal life, never to perish, and no one will snatch us out of Your hand

Amen

~WEDNESDAY~

Lamentations 5:10 "Our skin is as hot as an oven with the burning heat of famine."

Lord, we have a hunger. We have had it all of our lives

We have sought to fill it with work, with love

With beauty

With meaning

With friendships

With striving

With sound and with quiet

But all of our seeking and consuming has been a chasing after the wind

All streams run to the sea, but the sea is not full; to the place where the streams flow, there they flow again; all things are full of an unutterable weariness

Fill us with a vision, Lord: Of Jesus Christ who finished His work on the Cross; who set His face to Jerusalem, for our salvation, for love

Who shone forth out of Zion, the perfection of beauty

Who found His purpose in obedience to the Father's will

Who came eating and drinking, and they called Him a friend of sinners. Yet wisdom was justified by her actions

Who in the days of His flesh offered up prayers and supplications, with loud cries and tears, to the One who was able to save Him from death; and was heard because of His reverence

Who was oppressed and afflicted, yet He opened not His mouth

Whose flesh is true food, and whose blood is true drink. Lord, we want to see Jesus. Amen

~THURSDAY~

Lamentations 5:11 "Women are ravished in Zion, young women in the towns of Judah."

Sin is unspeakable, Lord. It is an affront to Your glory

It unravels the very fabric of this life we were created in

It violates the innocent

It destroys trust, does irreparable harm, exalts all that is vile and debased

It shatters beauty

It ruins hopes and dreams forever

But into this terrible despair the pure note of Your Gospel sounds among us

"Forever" is a word You have reserved unto Yourself

Sing, O barren one, break forth into singing. Break forth into singing and cry aloud! For more are the children of the desolate woman than of she who is married

Enlarge the place of your tent, do not hold back. Fear not, for you will forget the shame of your youth

For your Maker is your husband, the Lord of hosts is His Name; the Holy One of Israel is your Redeemer

For the Lord has called you, like a wife deserted and grieved in spirit. *"In overflowing anger for a moment I hid My face from you, but with everlasting love I will have compassion on you,"* says the Lord, your Redeemer

I will greatly rejoice in the Lord, for He has clothed me with the garments of salvation. Let us rejoice and exult and give Him the glory, for the marriage of the Lamb has come

His Bride has made herself ready, clothed in fine linen, bright and pure

Blessed are those who are invited to the marriage supper of the Lamb, His forever. Amen

~FRIDAY~

Lamentations 5:12 "Princes are hung up by their hands; no respect is shown to the elders."

Things are not as they should be, Lord. Age should be shown respect; rulers You have raised up should be given obedience

Supplications, prayers, intercessions, and thanksgivings should be made for all people: For kings and for all who are in high positions, that we may live a peaceful and quiet life, godly and dignified in every way

This is good, and it is pleasing in the sight of God our Savior, who desires all people to be saved and to come to the knowledge of the truth

For Your people have been lost sheep. The shepherds have led them astray, turning them away on the mountains. From mountain to hill they have gone; they have forgotten their fold. All who found them have devoured them, and their enemies have said:

"We are not guilty, for they have sinned against the Lord, the habitation of righteousness, the Lord, the hope of their fathers"

A voice! They flee and escape from the land of Babylon, to declare in Zion the vengeance of the Lord our God, vengeance for His temple

"A sword against the Chaldeans," declares the Lord, *"and against the inhabitants of Babylon."* For it is a land of images, and they are mad over idols

In those days and in that time, the people of Israel and the people of Judah shall come together, weeping as they come, and they shall seek the Lord their God

They shall ask the way to Zion, with faces turned toward it, saying, *"Come, let us join ourselves to the Lord in an everlasting covenant that will never be forgotten"*

And whom He did foreknow, He also predestined to be conformed to the image of His Son

In order that Christ might be the firstborn among many brothers. For from Him and through Him and to Him are all things. To Him be glory forever! Amen

~MONDAY~

Lamentations 5:13 "Young men are compelled to grind at the mill, and boys stagger under loads of wood."

Lord, has not man a hard service on the earth? Are not our days like the days of a hired hand?

We work tirelessly, but at the end of the day the thorns and thistles still grow in the fields. We strive for meaning, but futility still hovers ever before us like a flaming sword

We seek to have dominion, but all Creation rebels against us, just as we rebelled against You. We seek to multiply and cover the earth, but it is our kingdom we build, not Yours

We look up at the stars, and remember Your promise: *"So shall your offspring be"*

But it is the offspring of faith You were talking about, not that of works. As in water face reflects face, so the heart of man reflects the man

So when we see our reflection in Your holy Law, there is still much of the slave child, and not of the freeborn

For do we suppose that it is to no purpose that the Scripture says, *"He yearns jealously over the Spirit He has made to dwell in us"*

But You give more grace. Therefore it says, *"God opposes the proud, but gives grace to the humble"*

Let us submit ourselves therefore to God. Resist the devil, and he will flee from us. Let us draw near to God, and You will draw near to us. Cleanse your hands, you sinners, and purify your hearts, you double-minded

Be wretched and mourn and weep; let your laughter turn to mourning and your joy to gloom. Humble yourselves before the Lord, and He will exalt us

It is for freedom that Christ has set us free; stand firm therefore, and do not submit again to a yoke of slavery

Your people will offer ourselves freely on the Day of Your power, in holy garments

Amen, Lord

~TUESDAY~

Lamentations 5:14 "The old men have left the city gate, the young men their music."

Honor and beauty, Lord; we seek after them all our lives

Honor is like a mist on the hills, its mantle drawn over us by those who seek power. The fear of man lays a subtle snare, so easy to fall into. Who would not be thought well of? Yet that was not Christ's way

As One from whom men hide their faces, You were despised, and we esteemed You not. But in the heat of the day the mist vanishes away, and we find we have trusted falsely

How can we believe, who seek honor one of another, and seek not the honor that comes from God only? So cursed is the man who trusts in man, and makes flesh his strength

And what of beauty? So irresistibly our hearts are drawn to it

You found us in our infancy cast out on the open field, abandoned, left alone. You said to us in our blood, *"Live!"* You made us flourish like a plant of the field

You clothed us with embroidered cloth and shod us with fine leather; You adorned us with ornaments and put bracelets on our wrists and a chain on our neck. You put a beautiful crown on our head and adorned us with gold and silver; You gave us fine flour and honey and oil to eat

We grew exceedingly beautiful and advanced to royalty; our renown went forth among the nations because of our beauty, for it was perfect through the splendor You had bestowed on us

But what did we do with our beauty? We were unfaithful to You, on every high hill and under every spreading tree, and brought wrath and jealousy on ourselves. Yet You took the curse of all our falseness, and You bore the penalty for all our unfaithfulness

And we received mercy for this reason: That Jesus Christ might display His perfect patience as an example to those who would believe in Him for eternal life

To the King of the Ages, immortal, invisible, the only God, be honor and glory forever and ever. Amen

~WEDNESDAY~

Lamentations 5:15 "The joy of our hearts has ceased; our dancing has turned into mourning."

L*ove is the flower of life,* Lord; *it blossoms unexpectedly, and without law."* So we tell ourselves in the words of the godless poet

The prophecy of one whose eye sees clearly; the song of him who was hired to curse the tents of Jacob. Balaam son of Beor, who loved gain from wrongdoing

Rebuked for his own transgression in forsaking the right way and leading them astray; restrained in his madness by a speechless donkey, who spoke with human voice

And the depraved old seer lifted up his eyes and gave his oracle: *"I see Him, but not now; I behold Him, but not near. A star shall come out of Jacob, and a scepter shall rise out of Israel"*

For Love came down and was born of a virgin, that quiet night in Bethlehem: The Desire of the Nations, who would fill God's House with glory

And an angel of the Lord appeared to them, and the glory of the Lord shone around them, and they were filled with great fear. And the angel said, *"Fear not, for behold, I bring you news of great joy that will be for all people"*

A love that was not the flower of life, but its great and abiding Root

A love that was the Consolation of the world, a sign appointed for the falling and rising of many

A love that kept the holy Law from birth till death, perfectly, trustingly

The days have come when the Bridegroom is taken away from us, and in them we mourn

So also we have sorrow now, but we will see Him again, and our hearts will rejoice; and no one will take our joy from us.

Blessed are those who bless You, O Lord God of the Ages; and cursed all who curse You

Amen

~THURSDAY~

Lamentations 5:16 "The crown has fallen from our head; woe to us, for we have sinned!"

Our heart was proud, Lord. We said, *"I am a god; I sit in the seat of the gods, in the heart of the seas"*

Yet we were but men, and no god; though we made our heart like the heart of a god

We were indeed wiser than Daniel! No secret was hidden from us

By our wisdom and understanding we made wealth for ourselves, gathering gold and silver into our treasuries

By our great wisdom in our trade we increased our wealth, and our heart became proud in our wealth

Therefore thus says the Lord God: *"Therefore behold, I will bring foreigners upon you, the most ruthless of the nations; and they shall draw their swords against the beauty of your wisdom, and defile your splendor*

"They shall thrust you down into the pit, and you shall die the death of the slain in the heart of the seas. Then you will know that I am the Lord God"

And into this terrible curse Jesus Christ entered in for us, an innocent sacrifice for our sake

Foreigners drew swords against the beauty of His wisdom, and defiled His splendor

They thrust Him down into the pit, and He died the death of the slain, and the waters of judgment went over His head

And we looked upon Him we had pierced, and we knew that surely this was the Son of God

Behold the Lamb of God, who takes away the sin of the world

We have seen and have borne witness that this is the Son of God. Blessed be His Name

Amen

~FRIDAY~

Lamentations 5:17 "For this our heart has become sick; for these things our eyes have grown dim."

Lord, You have spoken in Your hot jealousy, because the enemy said of us, *"Aha!"* And said, *"The ancient heights have become our possession"*

Who gave Your land to themselves as a possession with utter contempt, that they might make its pasturelands a prey

Because they made us desolate and crushed us from all sides, so that we became the talk and evil gossip of the people

Therefore, O mountains of Israel, hear the Word of the Lord God:

Thus says the Lord God to the mountains and the hills, the ravines and the valleys

To the desolate wastes and the deserted cities, which have become a prey and derision to the rest of the nations all around:

"You, O mountains of Israel, shall shoot forth your branches and yield your fruit to My people Israel, for they shall soon come home

For behold, I am for you. I will turn to you, and you shall be tilled and sown

I will sprinkle clean water on you, and from all your idols I will cleanse you, and I will give you a new heart, and a new Spirit I will put within you

I will remove the heart of stone from your flesh, and give you a heart of flesh

I will put My Spirit within you, and cause you to walk in My statutes and obey My rules

You shall dwell in the land that I gave your fathers, and be My people, and I will be your God"

And the earth shall be full of the knowledge of the Lord, as the waters cover the sea. None shall hurt or destroy on all Your holy Mountain

Amen, Lord. Let it be

~MONDAY~

Lamentations 5:18 "For Mount Zion which lies desolate; jackals prowl over it."

The light of glory has faded, Lord; the Word became flesh and tabernacled among us

And we have seen His glory, glory as of the only Son from the Father, full of grace and truth

But the word You have pronounced over Your covenant people is *Ichabod:* The glory of the Lord has departed from Israel

Silence has replaced singing; sadness has replaced joy

Loss has replaced fullness; solitude has replaced the throng

Grief has replaced celebration

Until we go back to the beginning, to our first love

I said, *"Let me remember my song in the night; let me meditate in my heart"*

Your way, O God, is holy. What god is great like our God? You are the God who works wonders; You have made known Your might among the peoples

Then I said: *"I will appeal to this: To the years of the right hand of the Most High"*

If the light of the glory has faded, it was not He who first departed; it was we. Our sin has separated us from our Maker, our Husband, our Redeemer, our Friend

Return, O Israel, to the Lord your God, for we have stumbled because of our iniquity. Great is the Lord, and greatly to be praised in the mountain of His holiness

Beautiful for situation, the joy of the whole earth, is Mount Zion, city of the great King

We will tell the next generation that this is God, our God forever and ever. He will guide us forever. Amen

~TUESDAY~

Lamentations 5:19 "But you, O Lord, reign forever; your throne endures to all generations."

Lord, who is like You in all the earth? There is none holy like the Lord, for there is none besides You; there is no rock like our God

God reigns over the nations; God sits on His holy throne. Great is the Lord, and greatly to be praised in the city of our God!

We have thought on Your steadfast love, O God, in the midst of Your temple

Father of the fatherless and protector of widows is God in His holy habitations

Your way, O God, is holy. What god is great like our God?

Who among the heavenly beings is like the Lord, a God greatly to be feared in the council of the holy ones, and awesome above all who are around Him?

You have a mighty arm; strong is Your hand, high Your right hand. Righteousness and justice are the foundation of Your throne; steadfast love and faithfulness go before You

The Lord reigns; let the peoples tremble! He sits enthroned upon the cherubim; let the earth quake! Exalt the Lord our God; worship at His footstool! Holy is He!

The Lord of hosts is exalted in justice, and the Holy God shows Himself holy in righteousness

For your Maker is your husband, the Lord of hosts is His name, and the Holy One of Israel is your Redeemer, the God of the whole earth He is called. The Lord bless you, O habitation of righteousness, O holy hill!

You are the Christ, the Son of the Living God. Who will not fear, O Lord, and glorify Your Name? For You alone are holy. All nations will come and worship You, for Your righteous acts have been revealed

At once I was in the Spirit, and behold, a throne stood in Heaven, with One seated on the throne

He who testifies to these things says, *"Surely I am coming soon."* Amen. Come, Lord Jesus!

~WEDNESDAY~

Lamentations 5:20 "Why do you forget us forever, why do you forsake us for so many days?"

Lord, this world is full

Full of sound, full of activity, full of accomplishment

Moving, striving, taking advantage, avoiding, appearing, doing, living

Eating and drinking, marrying and giving in marriage

Why then do we find it so deeply, terribly empty? The sounds fade; all the work dies away

All the achievements crumble into dust, dust that passes away with the wind

All the doing comes to an end, and then begins again

All things are full of weariness, an unutterable weariness; a man cannot utter it

Remind me once again that the emptiness is anything that is not built on the foundation of Christ

That the weariness is as I have not turned to You for my strength

That a Day is coming when our Lord will return. And I must stay awake, for my salvation is nearer now than when I first believed

Show me once again that Jesus was forgotten and forsaken on the Cross for my sake

That while this world is indeed empty, crumbling, weary, vanity of vanities

Yet You have made known to me the path of life; in Your presence there is fullness of joy; at Your right hand are pleasures forevermore

My soul waits for the Lord more than watchmen for the morning; more than watchmen for the morning

Remember Your mercy, O Lord, and Your steadfast love, for they are from of old. Amen

~THURSDAY~

Lamentations 5:21 "Restore us to yourself, O Lord, that we may be restored! Renew our days as of old–"

G*reatly have they afflicted me from my youth"–*

Let Israel now say–*"Greatly have they afflicted me from my youth, yet they have not prevailed against me*

"The plowers plowed upon my back; they made long their furrows"

I go back, Lord, and I sift through the pieces. All the fragments of what once was:

The gladness, the companionship, the abundance

The victory

So easy it is to assign blame; so tempting to tear others' words and deeds to shreds

Reducing them to that one foolish statement, that one thoughtless action they committed. Yet Your Spirit reminds me that my guilt of sin was surely equal to theirs

And I do what one should with suffering and loss: Bear it, and compare it with Christ's:

Who was afflicted by His brothers without cause

Who was called the Man of Sorrows

Who was left alone when all His followers scattered

Who did not have a place to lay His head

Who suffered the ultimate defeat, death on the Cross

Lord Jesus, by Your sacrifice You have restored us to Yourself and renewed our days

By Your wounds I am healed, that I might die to sin and live to righteousness. Amen

~FRIDAY~

Lamentations 5:22 "Unless you have utterly rejected us, and you remain exceedingly angry with us."

Sin causes lasting damage and sorrow, Lord

O great and awesome God, who keeps covenant and steadfast love with those who love and obey You: We have sinned and done wrong and acted wickedly and rebelled, turning aside from Your commandments

We have not listened to Your servants the prophets, who spoke in Your Name to our kings, our princes, and our fathers, and to all the people of the land

To You, O Lord, belongs righteousness, but to us open shame, in all the lands You have driven us to, because of our treachery against You, as at this day

All Israel has transgressed Your Law and turned aside, refusing to obey Your voice. The holy Law requires that its curse and oath be poured out upon us

Only a sinless sacrifice could have paid for all this wrong; only a willing, innocent Lamb could have taken on Himself all the damage we did

Only for the joy set before Him did Jesus Christ absorb all Your righteous wrath on the Cross, for without the shedding of blood there is no forgiveness of sins

Only Your beloved Son could have canceled the record of debt that stood against us with its legal demands. This He set aside, nailing it to the Cross. Hallelujah!

Worthy are You to take the scroll and open its seals, for You were slain, and by Your blood You ransomed people for God from every tribe and language and people and nation!

He who was seated on the throne said, *"Behold, I am making all things new."* Also He said, *"Write this down, for these words are trustworthy and true."*

He took the cup of God's righteous wrath, and He drained it to its dregs. And He offered His very self to us, saying: *"This is My blood of the covenant, which is poured out for many for the forgiveness of sins"*

Jesus, You are our great and lasting hope. Show us Your glory in the Word today, and by the Gospel bear us up until that Day when we will drink of this cup with You new in the Father's Kingdom. Amen. Come quickly, Lord.

LightPath Publishing
100 S. Lynnhaven Drive
Staunton, VA 24401

lightpathpublishing@gmail.com

Psalm 119:105

www.ingramcontent.com/pod-product-compliance
Lightning Source LLC
LaVergne TN
LVHW091326150826
845673LV00006B/1779